Simon Reeve

first investigated the millennium bomb problem for The Sunday Times of London where he was one of the youngest-ever staff writers. He worked for the news, features and investigation departments for nearly five years before leaving at the end of July 1996 to complete this book. He writes for several British and European magazines, and has started writing his first novel. He is single and lives in London.

Colin McGhee

was a freelance journalist for many years and wrote for British magazines and national newspapers before starting his own magazine publishing business which specialised in satellite and cable broadcasting. After selling the firm, he set up his own consultancy company which worked in the forefront of computer and satellite developments. He is married with two children and lives in London.

VISION Paperbacks

Simon Reeve and
Colin McGhee

THE MILLENNIUM BOMB

Countdown to a £400 billion Catastrophe

First published in Great Britain in October 1996 by VISION Paperbacks, a division of Satin Publications Limited.

VISION Paperbacks,
a division of
Satin Publications Limited
3 Neal Street
Covent Garden
London WC2H 9PU
Email: 100525.3062@compuserve.com

Cover design: Justine Hounam.
Illustrations, front cover and text: Dave Brown.
Graphic, back cover: John Lund
Typesetting and design: Pixel Press.
Printed and bound in Great Britain: The Bath Press, Bath.

ISBN: 1-901250-00-8

**Dedicated to our family,
friends and contacts
for their
support and advice.**

Contents

Illustrations

THE BOMB IS PRIMED

Back in the dusty 1950s, the decade that saw the birth of the modern computer age, scientists unwittingly left an electronic time-bomb for future generations. The boffins were computer pioneers, playing with a new science that had grown out of the code-breaking machines used during the Second World War to defeat the Nazis. In a post-war era of science-fiction and travel to the stars, many became obsessed with creating computers that could function as humans or simply replace them. With their judgement clouded by the belief that science would advance quickly and replace the machines they were building in only a few years, these pioneers developed technology with a simple, standard flaw that is now ready to explode within thousands of computers around the globe.

The first and second generations of computer boffins listened to the ticking of the millennium bomb and became comfortable with the sound. It was almost hypnotic, and the new-fangled computers could do so many clever and wonderful things that the boffins never stopped to think what would happen to their creations at the end of the century.

The 1950s and the 1960s were an era of rapid scientific advances; new inventions were made all the time and it is not surprising scientists who were busy imagining robots and space-travel could not foresee that some of their basic early creations would last for years. But the pioneers made the rules, and set the standards that were to be used by the rest of industry for decades to come.

Even if one or two of them realised they might be installing a 'bomb', they must have convinced themselves it would never explode. Perhaps they thought that computers in the future would be such clever, powerful machines that they would be able to repair themselves in the event of problems. As this book shows, nobody took responsibility for curing the glitch, secure in the belief that the machines and the software of those days would not be in use a few decades later. But they were wrong. Some of the computers developed during the early decades of the technology are still in use in the late 1990s. The fatal flaw, in the shape of a timing defect, was even incorporated into the recognised software standards.

Although powerful computers in the 1990s have been reduced to the size of a coffee table book, the earliest computers were as large as a living room and contained hot, glowing valves, as in an old wireless. Memory or computer information storage space within these machines was both limited and extremely expensive, and programmers 'cheated' by shortening commands to a minimum.

For a generation used to the food rationing of the post-war era, it was an easy enough concept to adopt. When 'rationing' was applied to dates, it meant that 1955 was shortened inside the computer clock to just 55. In turn, 1998 becomes 98. When this abbreviation was applied to the entire date it was represented as, for example, 21/07/58. This became the standard way of programming dates into computers.

For many of us it also became our normal way of writing dates with trusty pen and ink. Shortening the date became standard practice and most of the computer industry continued to use just two digits instead of four to signify the year. Even now some parts of the industry are still writing new software that uses just two digits to signify the year.

Because dates are used so often and recur so frequently in software, it seemed sensible to our early software engineers to use the two digit year abbreviation because it saved memory not once, but many times. Everyone knew it was the twentieth century – that went without saying.

After the war, that meant it would work for the rest of the century – half a lifetime away.

Take out your chequebook, then your credit or bank cards, and see how society is programmed to accept that we are in the 1900s. Unless your bank is remarkably forward thinking, the date section of your chequebook leaves a blank space on the line for you to fill out day and month of the cheque, and then it has a "19" with a blank space after it for you to insert the tens and units.

That chequebook will work for the years 1996, 97, 98 and 99. After that, if you have an old chequebook you will just have to cross out the "19" and replace it with a 20. And that goes for millions of receipt books and order pads around the world. Presumably, nearer the change of century, banks will start printing cheques without the "19". After the millennium date change, they will feel safe to print "20" knowing it will be valid for the next hundred years.

It is easy to throw away one chequebook and print another. But not computers. You cannot throw away the information they depend upon, and you cannot cross it out with the stroke of a pen. The glitch should have been fixed many years ago and the changes should have been made before the 1990s even began, before the vast mass of data accumulated became too much to change. But it wasn't.

Plastic cash and credit cards are a good example. They are a little more computerised, and much more intricately integrated into bank' computer systems than paper. They are generated by computer and handled by computer. But check the validity dates and you will notice a two digit date format, the one that takes it for granted that the "19" in the year section of the date can go unstated.

This book demonstrates such shortcuts will not work for much longer. Most cards are now valid for two or three years. So banks will have to make major computing changes during the life of your current card if you are to be able to withdraw money and purchase goods beyond 1999. It is that close.

COMPUTERS need to know the date. A clock governs every computer in the world. Not only does every machine from a mainframe to a lap-top have a quartz crystal which keeps time – just like many watches – but it has a mathematical representation of time in every piece of software which needs to refer to the date. And that, with a few exceptions, means almost every piece of software in existence. For most computers knowing the date and being able to work using a calendar is a crucial part of their operation.

Computers used for industry and commerce need a clock to schedule electricity supply to meet demand, to organise buses and trains, to make social security payments and tax demands, to transfer credits between banks and to deliver blood supplies to hospitals on specific days of the week. They need the date to run spreadsheets, word processors, generate invoices and make slide presentations. They need it to run radio and TV transmission networks and editing studios, newspaper offices and the stock market, and to access employment records, police records, medical and insurance records.

In short, computers need clocks to run our lives and our countries. Unfortunately the two-digit date format clock stops working on 31st December 1999. Every time-bomb has a clock. This time-bomb is a clock.

Chapter One

OUR NUMBERS ARE UP

The millennium bug which has infested our computers is a problem of almost unbelievable simplicity, but it is confounding companies and astonishing politicians. The way computers tell the date is causing chaos on an international scale and could be the most expensive error humans have ever made.

The bugs become 'the Bomb' as we get towards the end of the century. Consider what will happen when we pass through 1999 towards the year 2000. If computers are shortening the date, their clocks will tell them it is the year 99. The next year is therefore the year 00. As millions of people around the globe party the night away on New Years Eve 1999 computer clocks will be happily ticking away, running our modern society and controlling everything from traffic lights and life-support machines to pension payments and missile controls. But as they tick past midnight many of the computers - up to 90% according to some estimates - will start to malfunction.; Some will think they have been tampered with and shut-down, while the majority will assume it represents the year 1900, the beginning of the twentieth century, and calculate dates accordingly.

As dawn breaks on New Year's Day over New Zealand and the rest of the South Pacific, the first area of the world to enter the new millennium, some experts warn that up to 50,000 mainframe computers around the world could be at risk of serious malfunction - a wonderful euphemism for shut-down, close or stop. Others warn that nearly everything containing a microchip will be at risk.

The potential for economic chaos is enormous. Many experts admit they are being conservative when they estimate that between one and five per cent of businesses could collapse because of the millennium bomb problem. Others have predicted that as many as 50 per cent of companies will not have fixed their computers and will in consequence face catastrophe.

The science of chaos theory teaches us what happens with a ripple effect, like a single drop of water falling into a still pond: the effects can be felt around the entire pond as tiny ripples spread across the surface. Chaos theory also teaches us that a butterfly flapping its wings in South America causes storms in Europe: the tiny creature is the start of a chain reaction that alters global events. And so it is with this minor computer glitch. We believe the problem is much more serious than current thinking suggests, but even if we accept the estimate that perhaps only one per cent of businesses will fail, it will still be enough to cause a sudden economic crisis. The doomed businesses will all fail within a very short space of time, and as they collapse so their supply companies, clients and everyone else upstream and downstream in their chain of business will be harmed.

Those wondering how a simple date could cause any significant problems, the sort that affect daily life and routine, should consider how computers govern our lives. The humble traffic light is controlled by a computer which tells it when to turn green, amber and red. The length of time it allocates for each lane or road of traffic to pass through on green is decided according to a carefully formulated program imbedded deep within the computer which switches between the various colours according to the day of the week. Sometimes traffic going into town during rush-hour is given more green lights than at other times of the day or at the weekend. If the computer controlling traffic lights cannot tell the day of the week correctly it cannot operate properly and direct the flow of traffic. Result: gridlock.

But computers control much more than traffic lights. The millennium bomb could mean your building society generously adds '99' years of interest to your high-interest savings account. Unfortunately at the same time your bank may start charging 99 years of interest on your mortgage. Prison computers could suddenly calculate that murderers and rapists are eligible for parole having served considerably longer sentences than foreseen by the judge who appears to have convicted them '99' years previously. Every computer will react differently, but tests that are already being conducted by companies desperate to find a cure for the glitch have proved that many computers will simply work out the difference in years between 1999 and 1900 and calculate a giant leap of 99 years. Even the most advanced computer is only as good as the person or people who programmed it, and in many cases that could have been as many as a thousand programmers, each of them tapping away for several years to create their own tiny part.

A computer runs many different software 'applications' to do a variety of tasks, and each of these applications may involve many programs. All of them, like the programmers, are cogs, without any understanding of the full workings of the rest of their joint creation. With so many people needed to mesh together to create a highly technical system, it is hardly surprising that mistakes are made and glitches go unnoticed.

Worse, it is much more difficult to go back through it all and cure the problems, which is one of the main reasons for the appalling lack of action taken by computer companies in the years, and even decades, since this problem became known. Until recently computer companies made no attempt to purge the machines they were supplying to industry and the public of the glitch. The result of this, probably the most costly and ridiculous error in history, is now troubling leaders of governments and industry: "Centenarians could appear on primary school intake lists; all military and aeronautical equipment could be simultaneously scheduled for maintenance; thousands of legal actions could be struck out; student loan repayments could be scheduled as overdue; and 100 years of interest could be added to credit card balances". So says Ian Taylor, the British Minister for Science and Technology.

Taylor is the politician first given the task of organising the British Government's reaction to the millennium glitch and creating enough awareness of the issue for companies and industry to fix the problem without the need for legislation or government grants. He is also the man who woke up the European Union to the dangers by raising the year 2000 problem with one of the most senior EU Commissioners. "We could be facing an imminent catastrophe," he has warned.

Bill Gates, the founder of the computer company Microsoft and one of the world's richest men, also recognises the problem, even if he is a little unclear about the possible effects: "There will be a headache but how much pain it will cause remains to be seen," he said. "Errors could appear in the behaviour of software that computes interest, organises information chronologically or figures out a person's age. A computer could miscalculate your age and deny you retirement benefits. Inventory systems could order stock at the wrong time and in the wrong quantity. Financial deadlines could be missed." Some programs, admits Gates, may not be able to tell the difference between the years 1900 and 2000.

The American Department of Defense has also admitted to

possible catastrophic failures in weapons systems and defence control computers which not only guard the nation from attack by renegade states, but also order stocks of boots for the Marine Corps and check that F-15 fighter planes have been properly maintained and serviced. According to some of the most senior officials and politicians within the Pentagon, one of the most heavily computerised nations on earth faces an extraordinary challenge posed by its own computers.

It is a world-wide problem. Even the Japanese are affected. The Japan Information Service Industry Association, a trade organisation, established a committee at the end of May 1996 to try and find a solution headed by Ryuichi Kono, the vice-president of INTEC (a huge computer company). The association surveyed about 2,500 companies and 500 government departments and agencies, and discovered that just 10 per cent of them were even vaguely prepared for the problem. Most were completely unaware of the danger.

SOME EXPERTS estimate that anything up to 90% of computers globally could be seriously affected by the millennium. The Gartner Group, American experts in Information Technology with their head office in Stamford, Connecticut, has been publishing research on the topic since 1988 and estimate that 30% of computer applications will not be millennium compliant, or 'millennium-friendly' by the end of the decade.

That might not sound serious, but consider how integrated and inter-reliant our economies have become. Consider how industry depends on everything arriving on time for companies to stay in business. Companies not only rely on their clients paying bills on time, but they are increasingly dependent on suppliers providing parts and stocks. If one part of the economic machine fails, it will drag down other parts and other sectors that rely on proper timing and deadlines.

"The year 2000 date change poses one of the most significant challenges ever faced by the IT industry and will have enormous impact on business applications, package solutions and system software, even putting some companies at risk in their business," said Kevin Schick, research director for the Gartner Group as he testified before the 14-member American House of Representatives Subcommittee on Government Management, Information and Technology on Tuesday, April 16th 1996. "The bottom line is the year 2000 virus is the most devastating virus ever to infect the world's business and IT systems."

Even reading through the computer-speak and allowing for an element of hyperbole to have crept in to Schick's speech, and that of the British minister Ian Taylor and dozens of other experts, there can be little doubt that many in the industry are becoming extremely concerned by our preparations, or lack of them, for facing the year 2000 crisis. The world-wide cost of fixing the glitch will be vast. Anything between $300 and $600 billion, according to the Gartner Group. It is a vast sum, many times the annual gross domestic product of some medium-size countries, but according to many it is a price that must be paid if society wishes to keep its computers working after the dawn of the next century.

Those given the task of analysing the problem for their firms and finding some sort of workable solution are discovering the full meaning of the saying 'looking for a needle in a haystack'. There are numerous complications to the year 2000 problem that make it "quite the most intricate problem we have ever faced", according to the director of one leading Italian bank in Milan who has been nominally in charge of the firm's computers for several years.

"Our systems people have come and gone and not one of them ever mentioned the problem to me," he said. "I am a banker, not a computer technician, and I only learnt about the problem when I was talking to someone at a party. I suddenly wondered what would happen to our bank cards, which all have two digits on them. Then one of our younger computer technicians read a report in an English magazine on the year 2000 glitch and investigated whether it would happen to us. He did a quick check, which then became a project, which has now had to become a time-consuming investigation of all our computers. We still have thousands of them to check but we have already found enough problems to keep us busy until the year 2050. It is by far the greatest challenge we have ever faced. I dread the end of the decade."

Computers are all controlled by sets of commands buried deep within the central processing unit, the brain of the machine which tells it what to do when it is turned-on at the mains, what to do when a user presses a button, and what to do when the owner tries to use a specific application like a word-processor. The commands are written in strange computer 'languages' with names such as COBOL, Unix and BASIC that require years of training for programmers to understand.

Each computer is controlled by lines and lines of these codes which in many computers are converted into binary numbers - represented by a series of zeros and ones. Anyone wanting to find the commands controlling the computer's dates cannot simply scan through a dozen or so lines of code and quickly make the changes. Lines of code can take up to several minutes to read through and identify simply because of the complexity of the language, its relationship to other lines, and the length of the line.

The language which controls each computer is especially important because some of the languages are so outdated there are fewer and fewer boffins or programmers left in the industry who can fully understand them - or if they do understand them they are not totally 'fluent' in the language. So computer experts are now writing special software which allows a computer itself to go into the lines of code and do the job automatically. As will be seen, this too, is not without its problems because the new 'search engines' cannot find all the millennium bugs.

The fact that they cannot all be easily found relates to the level of job satisfaction computer programmers often find in their jobs. Filling a computer with codes, and keeping an eye on them when they are operating, is often not the most exciting job or the one many of the operators hoped for when they were studying ways to create artificial computer life-forms or advanced computer technology. So the programmers have had a little fun over the years to alleviate the boredom. "I could not believe my eyes," said a computer expert at one of Britain's largest companies who has been given the job of fixing the glitch as the Millennium Project Manager. "We were looking through the most basic computer program in the company and stumbled across one date that had been 'hidden' under the date of a famous World Cup football final. As if we didn't have enough problems tracking down the dates, we realised that over the years some of the junior staff had been playing around with the computer and entered the commands to control the dates under different headings. That sort of tomfoolery would only become a problem if all the dates ever needed to be changed."

But now they do, and a company could change every single date in one of their computers in a bid to defuse the millennium bomb, only to discover after January 1st 2000 that the one crucial date they failed to change was the one hidden from their view under the name of a famous football match. A number of companies have found other 'hidden' dates by chance or line by line manual inspection. This laborious method, and running the debugged applications until they crash, then looking for the reason for the crash, is the only way of discovering them all. Computer 'doctors' have unearthed other vital date commands hidden under favourite birthdays, the names of husbands, wives, lovers and relatives, and other, rather more salacious headings.

The language may be impossible to understand in some computers or the date may not be in the 'right' place. But even if one embraces the positive thinking that will be necessary to defuse the millennium bomb in time, it is vital to consider another problem relating directly to the lines of code. There are just too many. If a computer is run on just a few hundred lines of code it could be checked and fixed in a couple of days. Unfortunately, no modern computer system is so simple; they may have hundreds or thousands of programs, each of which may contain hundreds or thousands of lines of code.

It is only by considering a large company that the full scale of the problem can be fully appreciated. Look at British Telecom, a major business which relies on computers; without them it cannot operate as a company. Across the whole of BT, in all its divisions and departments there are not just hundreds of lines of code that must be checked within the next few years; there are not thousands; there are in fact more than 100 million lines that must be laboriously scrutinised. It is a mammoth task.

The date bug has proliferated because time is of crucial importance within a computer. Every machine has an in-built master clock which counts the time from a fixed starting date. Signals recording the elapsed time since that date are generated by a quartz crystal vibrating at a fixed frequency and producing pulses at extremely accurate intervals. These pulses record the passing of seconds, minutes, hours and years and, using appropriate software in the computer's operating system, they tell programs loaded into the computer's memory exactly what time it is. If the master clock software uses only two digits to record the year then, to record the century, it needs to be re-written to add two extra digits. However, when that problem is solved there are many others.

The programmes which take their cue from the clock must be able to read those four digits. There are a myriad lines of software code which refer to the computer's clock and then execute an operation when a certain time period is denoted. All of these lines of code will have to be changed to match whatever new clock code and time period are being used, otherwise the programs will fail.

Perhaps the only aspect of the millennium bomb problem that can be accurately predicted is the time left on the clock to winkle out all these bugs. At the time of writing there are just over three years left to find all the answers. This, as many are pointing out, is a project with an immovable completion date. No excuses will be accepted, it cannot be put off and it cannot be altered: December

31st 1999 is the date by which our computers must be fixed if we want to avoid disastrous consequences.

"If companies don't understand what could happen with the year 2000 problem and react then they could have to suspend their business and that will have a massive economic and social impact," said Mili Lewis, the Millennium Program Manager for British Telecom, and the woman charged with the enormous task of fixing the computers at one of Britain's biggest organisations. "People can get cross about this but we simply have to get on with it and work to fix everything in time. The alternative is quite unthinkable."

AS WE SHOW later, governments now accept that a millennium meltdown is a serious possibility, so why has there been so little to read about it until recently? There is a dangerous belief that this is a science fiction story dreamt up by the computer world to make money, or that it may only have temporary effects. Most pervasive is the belief that the computer industry has been mobilised to combat the threat and is now completely in control. Supposedly, all the remedial fixing work is well in hand and the threat can be easily resolved by the experts.

But the people issuing this message are themselves part of the computing industry. Since they are specialists, the media tends to believe them, but their track record is far from impressive. These experts have known about it for years without doing anything to solve the problem and some manufacturers continue to sell machines that contain the fault.

So far the media has largely reported the topic as a computer story, regarded by news editors of newspapers as boring, lacking the human interest that sells newspapers. The stories have been presented almost innocuously, characterised not as a serious threat but as a fascinating problem for the computer industry to grapple with.

The first large broadsheet European newspaper to spot the

story was the London-based Independent on Sunday. In 1994, under the headline 'Computers Stuck in 1900s' it explained some of the implications. The article quoted Peter Ambrose, representing a group of large users of IBM main-frames trying to find a solution: "Its a funny project," he said. "If companies do everything right they'll expend a huge amount of effort and nobody will notice a thing. But if they get it wrong the consequences will be horrific. It's lucky the first day of the new century is a Saturday; programmers will have a weekend to work out temporary fixes".

Only a weekend for fixes? Such comments inoculate us against any real sense of alarm or urgency. In contrast, analysts now predict that the programmers available, working intensively for those companies which are first to recruit them, will not have time to finish the task. A few papers have begun to realise the potential impact and disruption.

THE SUNDAY TIMES of London was one of the first to devote serious column inches to the time problem in June 1996. Its "Focus" report, co-written by one of the authors of this book, was headlined "Millennium Meltdown - why are so many of our supposedly sophisticated computers unable to cope with a simple date change?". The article prompted further discussion of the problem, but even as this book goes to press there has been and remains a credibility gap. Even after the possible effects are explained logically and justified rationally in detail, people refuse to accept the inevitable conclusion that there could be widespread - unique - failures of almost every computer system we depend upon.

Yet as we disclose, the most knowledgeable experts are saying entire computer operations within companies, institutions and governments may simply have to be abandoned. They comprise a group which for more than three years has tried to confront the problem, and which has come to the conclusion that society must prepare itself, not to avoid a computer collapse but to deal with the consequences of a crash that is now unavoidable.

COMPUTER journalists depend for their livelihood on computers, and their perception is conditioned by the constant market expansion the industry has enjoyed. Most harbour the expectation that all problems must be solvable. Software is being constantly upgraded and fixed. They see the Year 2000 problem as a boost for the industry. The development will create extra work for programmers and new jobs for millennium bug consultants.

There is however, a different type of media within the computer world: the specialist report and the exchange of electronic mail between technical experts. These reports are important because they have been produced by individuals at the sharp end, who have gone much more deeply into the subject matter and examined in detail and at first hand the scale of the work which would be required to fix the millennium bug. The reports do not have a wide circulation and some are confidential. But the same worrying opinions can be seen exchanged between experts on Internet mail, and in their specialist discussion groups. At this level there in acceptance that every programme and system cannot be fixed.

During 1994 and most of 1995, a few prophets of doom tried to attract attention, but only a handful listened. During the latter part of 1995 and 1996 they started to get through to small numbers of decision makers, first in the United States, and then in Great Britain. But few computer industry reports or government analyses reflect the insider message that emerges daily with greater clarity: a total fix of the millennium bug will prove impossible.

We have seen before how official denials and assurances can hoodwink the media. It happened with Mad Cow Disease (BSE) and you can argue that it is happening with Mad Computer Disease - the millennium bug. The parallels are worth examining if only to make us wake up and question the assurances of experts.

British readers will recall what tactics were employed to allay worries about BSE and the safety of beef. There was the picture opportunity of a Government minister coaxing his daughter to eat a hamburger. For years the British Ministry of Agriculture assured the public the meat was safe. And then people started dying and tens of thousands of animals were sent for slaughter.

In the same way that only a minority of computer scientists accept the possibility of a fully-blown millennium disaster, only a handful of doctors and biologists had the courage to go public with the theory that BSE could cross over into humans. The millennium bug affects machines not cattle, but its evolution as a news story and topic of conversation is undergoing the same life-cycle. People should be worrying, now, about the cost of remedial work which has been put at hundreds of billions of pounds. Because when the chips are down, everyone will be affected.

Chapter Two

BIRTH OF A DREAM

The machines we have so recently created now threaten the very fabric of our societies. How have we reached this point? The answer may lie in the speed at which computers have developed. Only 50 years separate the earliest computers from the present 'wired' world.

Like current plans for the future, developments in the past were undertaken in a breathless rush in search of the possible. In the headlong dash, the millennium bomb has been overlooked; but, worse still, developments in the years ahead could put even more at risk. To put the problem in context we need to examine the development of computing and technology in the past and present, and explore our possible future.

The first machine that can really be called a computer was invented in 1833 by Charles Babbage, a professor of mathematics at Cambridge University. Resembling a giant abacus rather than a streamlined computer, the six-feet tall Difference Engine was a basic, huge calculating machine designed for producing mathematical and navigational tables, using a technique called the 'method of differences'.

Between 1847 and 1849, when Babbage was trying to build his 'baby', such tables were full of errors because they were generated by hand. Babbage thought machines could do the job much more quickly and more accurately than humans, just like a true computer pioneer. Unfortunately not everybody agreed with him and neither of his machines were actually built during his lifetime, partly because Babbage fell out with his engineer. Hindered by a lack of both understanding and funding, with most of his inventions uncompleted, Babbage died a broken man over 120 years ago. But the plans for his second computer, the 1847 Difference Engine Number Two, were saved for the nation, and in 1991 the Science Museum in London succeeded where Babbage had failed: it built and tested his invention for an exhibition to commemorate the bicentennary of the great inventor's birth. Using his original 20 drawings a two-man team working under Dr Doran Swade, the curator of computing at the museum, constructed the massive three-ton machine out of 4,000 bits of steel, bronze and cast iron.

The machine uses wheels and vertical rods which bob up and down and carry numbers from one column to the next whenever two of the numbers add up to more than nine. It is all highly complicated, yet when the machine's handle is turned the Difference Engine is able to calculate up to 30 decimal places. After months of testing, the two engineers, Barrie Holloway and Reg Crick, finally cranked it into life and the Difference Engine turned out the seventh power of each number between minus 80 and plus 80 and then correctly calculated solutions for a seventh order polynomial equation. Doran Swade was "over the moon", and said it proved that Babbage had been right all along. The significance of the machine was recognised when a section of it came up for auction at Christies four years later and was sold for £176,750 - three times its estimate - to a museum in Sydney, Australia.

The first electronic computers were invented as code-breaking machines during the Second World War and played a crucial role in the Allied victory. Their inventors were for long the greatest unsung heroes of their age, though their exploits have been celebrated recently in television documentaries and Robert Harris's best-selling book 'Enigma'. Colossus, along with most of the work at the Allies' code-breaking centre at Bletchley Park in Buckinghamshire, remained secret for nearly 50 years, but recently details have emerged of the events at the wartime equivalent of GCHQ which give a fascinating glimpse of the aims of the early computer pioneers.

The Germans had their Enigma code machine, which was mainly used for the protection of tactical information, but they also had another level of codes which were used for protecting Hitler's top-secret communications and were encoded by a machine called Geheimschreiber - the 'secret writer'. To scramble each message the secret writer used 12 motors of different sizes, three times as many as the Enigma machine.

The secret writer was the most powerful encoder of its time, and the Germans believed its codes were utterly impregnable. The Allies would never crack their communications, they joked. Fortunately, however, the Germans blundered in 1941 and accidentally sent a single message twice in a manner that allowed the British code-breakers at Bletchley to read both the message and the way it was encoded. It was a crucial breakthrough, and by 1942 the Allies were reading the so-called top secret German 'Fish' communications by comparing their messages with incorrect transmissions.

Decoding the communications traffic was an extremely laborious pen-and-paper process however, and in September 1942 Max Newman, a Cambridge University maths genius who had joined the Bletchley team, suggested building a machine that would do

much of the work by mimicking the Germans' secret writer. Newman and Alan Turing, another mathematician now hailed as a key figure in the development of modern computing, realised that to operate such a machine the Allies would have to draw on the new science of electronics. Experts from the Post Office Research Station at Dollis Hill in London were called in to help create the Colossus machine. With its 1,500 valves and the ability to read nearly 25,000 characters every second, the machine was a godsend for Allied High Command, allowing them to read thousands of top-secret Nazi messages, such as the signals Hitler was sending to his generals in the days before the D-Day landings in June 1944.

Although its power could be stored in a modern micro-chip, Colossus was a work of genius that played a decisive role in shortening the war, if not actually helping to decide its eventual outcome. It remained highly secret and was broken up at the end of the war along with other similar machines. Colossus, regarded

Manchester University's Mark-1 computer, built in 1948, was the first in the world to use a 'stored program' or what became known as software.

The banks of valves on either sides of the room had a processing power of one of today's simplest calculators.

In those days using four digits to denote the date was regarded as an extravagant use of memory.

as the godfather of modern computers, was only recently declassified, and a model has been reconstructed by enthusiasts including Tony Sale, a former intelligence officer.

In America, meanwhile, boffins were building their own computers during the mid-1940s. The first modern 'general-purpose all-electronic computer', the Electronic Numerical Integrator and Computer (ENIAC), was designed to compute ballistics tables for the army. It was enormous - 80 feet long and 18 feet high - weighed 30 tons and contained 17,468 vacuum tubes and 500 miles of wiring. At the time, it was a revelation because it could work at a speed of several hundred multiplications per minute, but because ENIAC's program was actually wired into its brain, anyone wanting to change the way it operated had to get out their pliers and rewire the entire machine. Oddly enough, such drastic action is not entirely dissimilar to the methods that must now be used to save thousands of computers around the world from the millennium bomb.

The Second World War proved to be the engine for the development of computers and computing, and in the Cold War era that followed the military likewise underwrote almost every major technical advance, including magnetic core storage, transistors and the silicon chip. Governments were the other main customers for the new computer companies that sprang up: public servants flocked to computer displays and rubbed their hands with glee as they realised that automation was on the way for thousands of bureaucratic tasks.

The first wave of computers continued to be large and unwieldy, with much of the computer's operating system and storage intricately connected to the hardware used. As the industry developed, memory, storage and software would take on many different forms before arriving at today's powerful desktop computers.

Since the 1940s there have been three watershed developments in computer electronics. In the 1950s valves were replaced by transistors; in the 1960s transistors were replaced by integrated circuits (which were really just small groups of transistors connected together); in the 1970s the microchip arrived. Microchips carry tiny electronic circuits allowing electronic signals to travel around the machine telling the computer what to do; they also store the signals within the computer so that information can be processed much more speedily.

Known commonly as 'chips', they are mass-produced quickly and cheaply on thin discs of silicon and are the main reason why today's computers are such small machines capable of handling millions of instructions per minute. The big development of the 1980s was an enormous increase in the power of the chip: combined with the launch of dedicated software programmes and new operating systems, they have brought about the personal computer revolution.

If chips made small personal computers possible in the home, it was because they had already taken over the office. The business computing power which required a roomful of mainframe machinery in the late 1970s now sits in a desktop machine. Once used only by specialised VDU (Visual Display Unit) operators, they were 'dumb' terminals dependent upon the central unit to store and process information.

The first personal computers to hit the office desk were stand-alone machines, little more than an electric typewriter, but they contained their own storage, memory, intelligence and programs. It was the boom in companies writing programs, software applications to handle word processing and then accounting, that gave PCs a firm foothold in the office. As more and more software programs were written to handle every aspect of business documentation, they became indispensable.

A fundamental difference existed between old-style mainframe computing and personal desktop computing: the large old machines tended to have dedicated software written specially for 'big' jobs, where many operators needed to be connected to a central system, whereas desktop machines allowed workers to carry out more general tasks on a single independent machine, using mass-produced software. In the last five years, however, that distinction has narrowed as the PC systems have been increasingly linked together in networks. Still able to operate and store work independently, they share software and communicate with each other via a powerful 'server' unit.

Each desk worker has therefore had to become a PC operator using a computer that handles much of its own information. These may stand alone, but, increasingly connected in a network, they're everywhere. In the 1990s the main development has been this linking together of PCs in networks, both within and between companies. Hailed as the fastest growth business ever known, it is not surprising that the different types of construction used in the old mainframe computers have been largely forgotten or overlooked in the excitement of constant new developments – until the rude shock of the millennium bomb. It is these early systems, especially the ones with their customised operating systems and out-of-date software language, which pose most of the severe Year

2000 date problems today. Attention was being concentrated elsewhere, on the enormous advances in the PC world.

The desktop office computer was driven by the chip and convenient business applications, but games and entertainment were the forces pushing computers into the home. The first machines were computers with limited memory and speed, but sales really took off with the arrival of large, cheap, hard-drives for information storage, point-and-click mouse-based programs driven by Microsoft's Windows, and the CD-Rom. Add to this cocktail worldwide communications by modem for entertainment, information and business, and the sales of home PCs rocketed. We now have the world of the information superhighway, cybernauts, the Internet, e-mail, multimedia, and more gimmicks and peripherals than you can shake a hard-drive at.

The British in particular have been sold on taking the new technology into their homes for both business and pleasure, and according to research released in May 1996 the nation has become the home-computer centre of the world, with double the American level of ownership. Nearly one in three British homes have a computer (a total of 7.5 million computers), compared with one in five in France and Germany, and less than one in six in the United States. The report, by Olivetti Personal Computers, used government figures to conclude that average computer use in Britain now exceeds 10 hours a week and almost 45 per cent of homes with schoolchildren own a personal computer.

Politicians have been quick to jump on the 'information age' bandwagon. At the time the report was released, Britain's governing Conservative party and the opposition Labour party were competing in a battle to be seen as the greatest proponents of technology in the classroom. Both claimed to have the brightest vision of the future for information technology in schools and the greatest understanding of the needs of the next generation of computer-literate schoolchildren.

Tony Blair, the Labour leader, offered British Telecom a host of new commercial opportunities if they agreed to connect every school in the nation up to the 'information superhighway'. Robin Squire, the Conservative Education Minister, told the press that the government was already doing what Labour was promising to do when (or if) it was elected. In the US, President Clinton had long beaten both parties to it as his government made the information age and the superhighway its own political property.

In an age when one in three children never, or hardly ever, reads a book outside school, do the easy joys of computers and computer games risk taking over the minds of our young? Will there be a bright new world of technology where the book of old is a computer screen and a mouse is used to 'turn the page'? Even television watching has been drastically cut down by computer usage, and some children are spending up to 20 hours each week with their faces glued to a new type of screen - a computer terminal.

Peter Victor, writing recently in 'The Independent' newspaper of London, said that the home computer's status had been boosted to that of the hi-fi, with thousands of people buying a computer for their homes every day. Victor quoted the example of Nicholas James, an oil trader in Richmond, Surrey, his wife Georgina and their young children Fiona and Louisa (then aged 10 and six respectively).

They are a typical 'microchip' family, said Victor. Father uses the home computer, which is connected up to his office computer, and a personal lap-top portable machine to reduce the hours he works in his office, while his wife, a former journalist and self-confessed 'technophobe', uses the computer to access the Internet and write articles for a local magazine. The girls have apparently improved their maths and spelling by using 'educational games software'. Unfortunately the James family are the exception rather than the rule: Peter Victor points out that 54 per cent of users regularly play games on their computers.

The distinction between home and business computing is starting to blur, as much of the personal computing equipment and software becomes standardised. Computer networks within companies, and connections between companies, are linking with computers in the home. The 'wired world' concept means that communications are the current big development, linking millions of PCs and microchips.

This brings us up to the present, but computer developers are already leaping ahead with what they call the neural network. They believe the future of computing lies in modelling new computer circuits on the composition of the human brain. They want to build tiny computer networks which interact with each other and learn from their mistakes, creating neural networks by connecting up groups of special computer cells in a manner that crudely replicates the complex nerve networks in our brains, and teaching these networks to behave in a specific way: thus creating Artificial Intelligence (or AI). Such machines are supposed to dispense with the need for constant programming, so a technician no longer needs to keep re-writing computer programs to produce a specific result - the idea is that the machine could simply be re-started until it 'learnt' to produce the correct result desired by its operators. It would develop an autonomous intelligence of its own.

However, with more than 30,000 cells in a portion of human brain the size of a pinhead there are billions of possible connections in our brains. Neural information is channelled through tens of millions of cells and across the surface of our brains. We're amazing, and no computer has even come close to replicating our astonishing capacity for thought. But the boffins are certainly trying: in 1990 the Japanese Ministry of International Trade and Industry started a ten-year research project into neural networks that should - they hope - develop new ways for computers to replace human thought. They have a long way to go - scientists have not yet been able to create computers with a greater complexity of 'thought' than the equivalent found in many insects.

The principle of neural networks goes back to 1943, when Warren McCulloch and Walter Pitts, two American scientists, published the first paper which suggested building electronic circuits for computing basic equations, on a similar plan to nerve connections in the brain. In the 1960s scientists went off the idea of creating neural networks in the hope that they could use a cruder route to creating AI: jamming as much information as possible into a computer program and telling it that if 'this' happens, it should do 'that'. But in the 1980s and 1990s the idea of a neural net has re-emerged, driven by the massive growth in the power of computers over the last 30 years.

THE PUSH towards AI is dogged by the legacy of Alan Turing, the mathematician who worked with the code-breakers at Bletchley Park during the Second World War. In 1950 Turing published a paper in the philosophical journal 'Mind', entitled 'Computing Machinery and Intelligence'. It described a game that would, he said, decide whether a machine was truly artificially intelligent. The game is still a benchmark - or a black cloud, according to some scientists - in the world of AI, which has proved incapable of inventing a machine to pass what is known as 'Turing's test'. He proposed placing an independent judge in a room where he would ask questions of a computer and a person and not be able to tell from their answers which was the person and which was the machine.

Turing believed that future scientists would regard the true test of a computer as being whether it could be deemed intelligent in the human sense of the word. "I believe that at the end of this century the use of words and general educated opinion will have altered so much that one will be able to speak of machines thinking without expecting to be contradicted," he said. In recent years, scientists have questioned the virtues of the test, saying it is seeking an unrealistic computer intelligence.

Artificial flight (such as a jumbo jet) is not like natural flight (such as a bird), so why should artificial intelligence replicate human intelligence? It is more important, so they argue, that the computer should reach its own level of intelligence rather than that of a human. Even so, the majority of computer experts still seem to accept the relevance of Turing's test, and in 1991 the Loebner prize of £100,000 was put forward for any computer capable of fooling a judge into thinking it was a human. Nobody has collected the award - so far.

After the Loebner prize, a smaller contest was established for computers to discuss specific subjects, including, strangely enough, Burgundy wines. One machine, called 'PC Therapist', actually managed to fool half of the ten judges into thinking they were talking to a person with a banal level of conversation. Part of it went thus:

Judge: "Hello! You seem to be feeling quite witty today".

Computer: "Hello, judge, what is your mood today? Happy? Sad? Ready for some fun? Hello - how's the weather up there today? Let's talk about psychology".

Judge: "It has been a long day! Now I think I'm ready for some fun. The weather isn't very pleasant today. Do you have any jokes that could lift the clouds?".

Computer: "Everybody talks about the weather but nobody seems to do much about it. Why do you need to tell me now you think you're ready for some fun? Groannnnn..."

If the exchange seems contrived, that may be because many critics said the computer was programmed to use a number of tricks, such as avoiding the question, and 'turning' conversations back on the judges. When the PC Therapist III was shown at a conference in London some observers found it "rambling and erratic".

In response to a question from Heinz Wolff, the director of the Institute of Bioengineering at Brunel University, who asked whether the computer had slept well the previous night, the machine responded by saying "at night there is no such thing as an ugly woman". Another questioner asked the computer who its father and mother were and received the response: "God could not be everywhere so he created mothers...happiness is just around the corner...why do you ask?". Hardly a convincing performance.

Computers can be trained and programmed on a particular

topic or subject, but ask them to participate in an open conversation that flows from one discussion to another, and their wires start to melt. It is the same for artificially intelligent robots: they can be programmed to undertake specific tasks which are drummed into their memories, such as picking up a loaf of bread and slicing it into separate pieces for toasting, but a single robot that can simply meander around a house performing household chores is still a dream for the future.

Computers are already using what passes for AI in credit-card companies to monitor patterns of spending by their clients and spot potential fraud. Speech-recognition computers, handwriting and facial recognition machines - all use artificial intelligence. In June 1996 British Telecom scientists announced that they had devised a computer program called Netsumm which uses artificial intelligence to distil lengthy documents to just a few sentences while retaining the overall meaning.

In Switzerland, Professor Nadia Thalmann of the University of Geneva has been developing artificially intelligent computers that can tell when humans are happy or sad, and return emotions appropriately. In July 1996 she revealed her work at a 'Virtual Humans' conference in Los Angeles and told the audience that it is possible for the computer to recognise a user's emotions and voice, and for the machine to show shock and amusement. Her computers are using neural networks to look at how our facial muscles are changing the outline and structure of our face, and then following the same movements to warp a face on the computer screen. Such technology would open the way for banks, travel agents and shops to install more 'customer-friendly' technology that could include a monitor with a smiley happy face. The reader can decide whether that would be a technological 'advance' or merely annoying.

In the world of finance, the London Stock Exchange is using AI techniques to spot illegal insider trading and manipulation of share prices. The software, a 'hybrid intelligence system', is among the most advanced in the world, costs £500,000 and was developed by doctoral students in the Computer Science department of University College, London; it is capable of analysing all the Stock Exchange's data on share trading and uses AI to scan the information, picking out suspicious deals from a mass of figures. It works by replicating elements of human thought at high speed using a combination of neural networks, genetic algorithms and 'fuzzy logic'.

Fuzzy logic'? This is yet another strand of AI, and the source of many new technological advances such as the anti-shudder camcorder. Drawing on the philosophy of Zen, fuzzy logic dispenses with the simple black and white world of computing and accepts there are infinite shades of grey. Practically, this means that instead of following set rules or commands, a fuzzy logic computer behaves more like a human being. The best way to explain this is probably by analysing what happens when we spot a vaguely familiar face in a crowd: we search through our memory banks until we find the closest picture to put a name to the person. A normal computer will scan the face and then search through its memory asking specific questions with straight yes or no answers until it has built a picture that it could relate to the face it has seen in the crowd, while a fuzzy logic computer would work more like the human brain.

For other visions of the future we can turn to British Telecom and its research centre at Martlesham Heath in Suffolk which consistently makes revolutionary suggestions about the way our society could be heading. In January 1996, Professor Peter Cochrane, the head of advanced applications and technologies at the laboratory, announced that he believes computers will be 1,000 times faster in the early years of the next century than they are now, and computers as powerful as the human brain and capable of 10 million billion operations a second are not far off development.

To the surprise of many, Cochrane has also speculated that a new type of being or person might start to develop from these hyper-fast computers, which would not think like a human but might be able to suggest different ways of approaching problems to its human masters. Cochrane did not speculate how far we are away from the master becoming the servant.

Just eight months later one of Cochrane's prophecies seemed to be in the process of realisation. In August 1996, President Clinton announced plans to develop the world's most powerful computer for the simulation of nuclear tests by the end of 1998. The £60m supercomputer, to be built by IBM, will be 300 times more powerful than any existing computer, and capable of one trillion calculations per second.

The machine will be set up at the Lawrence Livermore National Laboratory in California, which is co-ordinating a $1 billion effort to produce computers capable of ten trillion calculations per second by 2004. US government scientists believe that only computers of such enormous power can mimic the actions of nuclear weapons and simulate explosions without the need for real bombs and violations of any future comprehensive nuclear test ban treaty.

Clinton's announcement was made as 61 delegates from around the world met in a bid to create a draft test-ban treaty that they could all agree upon and adhere to. Delegates from both China and India expressed fears that the computers could be used to develop new types of nuclear weapons, although this was dismissed by the Pentagon.

Scientists are even considering warping nature into a computing device as they design organic chemicals which can arrange themselves into complex electronic systems; using such 'natural computers' the equivalent contents of a medium-sized public library could be stored in a memory the size of a sugar cube. To speed up computers, scientists are working on optical computing, where calculations are carried out using rays of light rather than electricity, to massively increase processing power.

BT's boffins at Martlesham Heath are working to create electronic 'ants' that could live inside computerised telephone exchanges and try to keep them running smoothly by looking for faults and undertaking repairs. The 'ants' are in fact just figures in the software, but BT's Dr Jose-Luis Fernandez wants them to feed off electronic impulses, with the result that only successful repair 'ants' will live.

The race to get inside the human brain, or create an alternative brain, continues apace. One development, of considerable concern to those who believe computers are already quite dangerous enough, was revealed in 1994, when scientists at the American Naval Research Laboratory in Washington developed a way of attaching living embryonic brain cells to computer silicon chips. The scientists took the extraordinary step of taking the brain cells in a rat that are responsible for logic and memory functions and growing them on exactly the right spots on a microchip so they could connect up with neighbouring cells. Details of the research were released - probably accidentally - to a small specialist magazine, and the Pentagon was remarkably reluctant to discuss the implications of the 'bioelectronic' science, but with living brains having millions more possible connections than even the most advanced chips, the potential for living brain material to be used in computers is frightening, opening the way for thinking, living humanoids, just like something out of 'Star Trek'.

The linking of computers and the human brain may need no physical connection, say American scientists who announced, also in 1994, that they had developed a computer workable by the mind, allowing full mental communication between man and machine. The military love the idea. Nothing would please them more than to have superfast aircraft that could be operated by thought, such as that shown in the film 'Firefox', which starred Clint Eastwood as an American pilot who steals a prototype Soviet plane so fast it has to be controlled by thought. Users of the American system, called BrainLink, wear a hand-band connected to a normal computer and as brainwaves are picked up by sensors in the headband they are converted into digital information for the computer to read.

"Eventually we think the BrainLink systems will enable a quantum leap allowing humans and computers to operate as a virtual organism," said Richard Patton, the president of Advanced Neurotechnologies in interviews when the BrainLink was announced. The British Psychological Society annual conference was shown the potential of the system when they were presented with a computer with a red box on its screen, and asked to change it to a green box simply by using their brains.

According to Patton users can 'learn' what type of mental activity changes the colour, but many may question the wisdom of expecting humans to modify their behaviour to accommodate computers when the original point of the machines was that they would adapt to our behaviour.

A year before the BrainLink was announced, researchers at Fujitsu in Japan announced that they were also training a computer to pick up specific patterns in the brain. Electrodes attached to the side of the head could pick up 'silent speech', enabling keyboard operators to 'think' rather than type. In the race to break down the barriers between man and his machine, the team at Fujitsu were developing Superconducting Quantum Interference Devices (SQUIDS) which can pick up even the smallest amount of brain activity.

Leading experts predict that the SQUIDS could soon be so powerful that they would read a person's mind when they sit in front of a computer, or even by being in the same room as it. Link that sort of power into a defence or a security system and you have the ultimate Big Brother, an horrific Orwellian vision of the future. Scientists might well claim that the development would be of enormous use to help handicapped people, but it would also be a terrible weapon in the wrong hands - not just the ultimate lie-detector, but a mind-reader with enormous power to subjugate.

The use of powerful networked computers and communications for population control is already on trial in many different experiments around the world. In America and Europe, thousands of cameras have been installed in city streets, shopping malls and along highways to scan and read both vehicle number plates and human faces in crowds. The system will eventually allow the authorities to identify, search for, and track vehicles and people alike as massive computers compare databanks of information on individuals with the images the cameras are registering.

In Singapore, a trial involving personal smart cards allows them to open and close apartment doors, use bank cash machines, buy goods, travel on public transport and open and close workplace doors: linked to one giant computer, the card owner can be tracked every time the card is used. Meanwhile, an Israeli-developed system puts the smart card information into a miniature antenna which can be registered by any number of scanners strategically placed by the authorities without the user even using the card; in the EU a similar project aims to have all motor vehicles implanted with a similar device which will register each time the vehicle passes a scanning point.

The first scanning points are to be toll booths, with the system being sold as a convenient way to avoid the need to stop and pay tolls manually, but scanning points could eventually be installed on every kilometre of highway and at every city junction. In a hospital system under trial the first personal ID chips for humans are to be injected under the skin between the finger bones on the back of the hand, in the form of an information pellet which will remain there for life and be scanned at each medical visit - a technique already successfully tried with animals.

It does not require a genius to understand that with the planned leap in supercomputer calculations to trillions per second, and the parallel growth in communications, the wired society could eventually mean total population control by computers. Human mind readers, cyborg brain implants, information munitions, artificial intelligence, population monitoring, warping nature, and replacements for human beings: you might think that some of the concepts under development are dangerous and amoral, but they excite and enthuse computer developers.

Whether the developments are right or wrong are rarely made considerations. In the computing industry there is no stopping to think what may or may not be good for society. It is a feature of computer developers that they simply want to build anything they perceive as feasible, always leaping to the next level of possibility. This is despite the fact that computing has its problems right now with present systems, and it has always had its problems; but there has been no stopping to get them right, just a relentless runaway development. As we further explore the mistakes the industry has made with the millennium bomb, it is unpleasant to think what they could do with artificial intelligence. Which raises the fundamental question, can computing and the computer industry be trusted?

Chapter Three

WAKING THE POLITICIANS

The millennium bomb has been ticking for a generation but most politicians are only just beginning to realise the impact it could have on computers and everything they control. So far only a few forward-thinking politicians have realised the year 2000 crisis must be considered a matter of national and international importance; one that requires co-ordination at government level to find solutions.

A few State-sponsored task forces have been established in North America, Europe and Australasia to investigate the extent of the problem and report back with their findings as quickly as possible. But reporting on the problem is a long way from solving it. Even supposedly enlightened organisations like NASA are still slumbering.

Waking the Politicians

With the Gartner Group predicting a $600 billion bill for fixing computers world-wide, there is clearly no scope for complacency. A substantial slice of this bill will ultimately have to come out of government budgets as many of the most complex systems infected with the bug are government-owned. It will have direct political implications because none of this cost has been budgeted for. The money will have to be found either by cutting expenditure in other areas or by raising taxes.

In Britain, some experts believe the estimated cost to taxpayers of reprogramming or fixing computers could be more than £5 billion but at least there are signs the warnings have penetrated the highest levels of government.

The alarm was raised by Millennium UK, a firm of computer experts based in Bournemouth on the English south coast, who have quickly grown to become Britain's premier Year-2000 troubleshooter after linking up with an American firm who had already identified the market potential for fixing the bugs. Millennium UK's directors realised that Britain needed waking up to the impending crisis. There was more than enough work to keep the firm busy but, when they looked objectively at the implications, they realised the country was oblivious of a serious economic threat. So Brad Collier, Millennium UK's marketing director, arranged a meeting in Autumn 1995 with David Atkinson, the local Conservative Member of Parliament for Bournemouth East, and during a lengthy chat he explained the potential effects of the year 2000 on the British economy.

Collier says Atkinson was an instant convert, one of the few politicians to fully comprehend the damage that could result from the two digit date format within computers. The MP promptly set about raising awareness of the issue at Westminster. He began bombarding the Department of Trade and Industry with questions and scooped his fellow politicians when the Financial Times of London published an article.

On June 6th 1996, Atkinson raised the millennium bomb issue in the House of Commons with Ian Taylor, Minister for Science and

Ian Taylor MBE, MP, Britain's Science and Technology Minister. There could be a commercial collapse and international chaos, he says.

Technology. The debate started at 10pm and there were only a few MP's in the Commons to listen to the discussions. However the Bournemouth MP was able to place a vivid account of the problem and its consequences on the Parliamentary record. What he said is worth reporting in detail as it clearly helped to galvanise the Government into action.

"This is my second attempt to raise a matter that should concern everyone who has or uses a computer," said Atkinson as he started the debate. "It is one that will concern most businesses and all Government Departments, not just in this country but throughout the world. It is the effect that the change of date at the turn of the century, from 1999 to 2000, will have on computers. Quite simply, if they are not prepared, they will fail."

Atkinson went on to mention how the British media coverage of the problem had shifted from articles in the specialist computer press to stories in more mainstream daily and weekly quality newspapers. He said he had questioned the Prime Minister about the Year 2000 problem the previous December and sent written questions to every Government Department, including to the Minister for Science and Technology. He had also written to the Prime Minister.

"It appears that that I am the only hon. Member to pursue the matter thus far, and the publicity that I have provoked has produced expressions of relief that, at last, someone is doing something," said Atkinson. "I am pleased to have the opportunity tonight to enlarge on the problems, and I am sure that I am not the only one to look forward to the Minister's reply."

It was a friendly debate, devoid of acrimony. Clearly referring to Millennium UK, the MP went on: "A constituent came to see my at my surgery last autumn to share his concern that neither business nor Government appeared to be aware of, let alone ready for, the century date change. Even I was able to grasp the potential seriousness of the problem, and my initial inquiries confirmed that my constituent's fears were far from groundless.

"All but the most recent computers have been programmed to recognise a shorthand standard date format - dd/mm/yy - with two figures for the day, the month and the year. For example, my hon. Friend the Minister's date of birth would be given as 18/04/45. Because [computer] memory is or was very expensive, programmers economised by cutting out the first two digits of the year, 19, to save money and memory. Thus two-digit year dates exist on millions of data files used as input to millions of applications."

Atkinson said that this was the crux of the problem: "Those computers will recognise the double zero digits of 2000 as 1900. As a result, all calculations, logic and date-driven processes will fail to function properly at midnight on 1 January 2000." He then pointed out that if the minister's computer could not recognise the date change, it would show his age to be not 55, but minus 45. "I would not want that prospect for my hon. Friend," said Atkinson.

For the pathetically small number of politicians left in the House of Commons that night, Atkinson explained how each of them could check their computers for the millennium bomb: "All of us with personal computers can apply a simple test to see whether they will fail at the end of the century. We can set the date to 31 December 1999 and set the time to 23:58. We can switch off the computer and, after a few minutes, switch it back on to check the date. It should say 1 January 2000, but my computer said 4 January 1980. Some 95 per cent of all personal computers fail that test."*

Atkinson warmed to his theme: "The vast majority of our information systems are based on the original, faulty standard date format, which will cost billions of pounds to reprogram. One esti-

* The authors do not recommend people should try this test as some computers may not reset or files could be corrupted.

mate of the cost is put at £400 billion world-wide and £20 billion for this country alone; the cost to the United States Government will be $30 billion. Those costs are rising daily, as the shortage of skills available to undertake the necessary reprogramming and recoding is realised.

"There can be no doubt that, unless organisations are prepared and have taken the necessary action, they will face catastrophic consequences, including a disastrous loss of trade and revenue - it is no exaggeration to say that some of them may go out of business very early in the new century. Many of them will have experienced a minuscule taste of what is to come on 29 February this year, as some computers did not recognise the extra leap year date. A piece of medical equipment in a hospital failed to work on that day."

According to Atkinson the consequences of what might happen are wide-ranging and threaten the competitive position of many exporting countries unless they have anticipated the problem in time. Atkinson painted a dire picture: "Supermarket computers will fail to replenish stocks and will throw out existing stocks, calculating that everything will have gone mouldy on the shelves after more than 99 years. The time locks of buildings will be unable to recognise the correct date, so staff will be locked out and vaults will be open."

He also told the House the nightmare consequences for national and international travel: "Trains will not run because their control systems will be unable to say what else is on the track that day. Flights will be cancelled as computers in airport maintenance will have grounded all aircraft because they are 99 years overdue for overhaul."

He said if that was not enough there are also the consequences for the computers of Government Departments and agencies "unless they have been properly prepared", the most obvious being the automatic payment of benefits systems and pay-as-you-earn that generates millions of tax returns. "Such a computer failure would affect our system of court orders, the child support maintenance system and car licence expiry dates. Traffic lights and school bells will operate their weekday schedules. Libraries will send out notices of fines for some seriously overdue books, and any program that prints a date on a cheque or invoice will stop working properly.

"The potential for disaster lies most in the financial sector. The interdependency of computers and the complex computer systems used in all financial transactions will create huge problems for City institutions. Even if their own systems have been reprogrammed and are working correctly, other firms with which they are dealing may not have had the same foresight."

He gave an example: "A firm may be awaiting the processing of a derivatives contract in Singapore which, if not correctly processed, may undermine that firm's short-term liquidity. The huge sums that are transferred every day in settlement of bond, equity, trade or foreign exchange flows bring the danger of a systemic breakdown of the banking settlements system, which could lead to temporary liquidity crises and perhaps bank failures."

It was frightening stuff and, as we shall see, not much of an exaggeration. London is the centre of the global financial services industry, Atkinson said, adding that it is vital that the UK takes a lead on this issue. "Most major financial institutions will, I hope, have their systems in order on time, but inter-relation of the industry means that all firms will have to be made aware of the seriousness of the problem."

Addressing the science minister directly, the MP asked: "What assurances or policy proposals has my hon. Friend received from the Bank of England, the London stock exchange, city regulators and the European central bank to prepare the markets for 2000?" According to Atkinson, Britain is a more sophisticated information technology market than the rest of Europe, and continental European companies are in a worse position than Britain in making preparations and planning for the year 2000 glitch. He wanted to know whether Britain could gain some financial rewards by exporting computer experts abroad to solve millennium problems in foreign companies.

Atkinson said in May 1996 he had tabled written questions to every Government Department (by which MP's can extract information from the Whitehall machine) to find out how they were responding to the problem. He said he was encouraged to learn that most Departments seemed to have an awareness, "but not all are treating it with the seriousness that it deserves".

According to the MP many of the replies he received showed undue complacency. "I hope that their confidence is justified and that, with the advice of the Central Computer and Telecommunications Agency - (the CCTA is the main advisor to the British government on the year 2000 problem as it relates to state organisations) - and computer suppliers, they will be prepared for the century date change."

Public sector computer systems are, in general, older and larger than similar systems in the private sector, and Atkinson wanted to know what the government minister's understanding was of the percentage and the number of Government computers that need to be reprogrammed or replaced, and the estimated cost. A recent survey by Taylor's department had apparently revealed a high level of awareness amongst information technology directors.

The MP questioned whether such a claim squared with newspaper reports that only eight per cent of businesses have conducted an audit to assess the extent of the risk, and more than 90 per cent are failing to deal with it. He went on: "As one of the essential messages seems to be that the chain is only as strong as its weakest link, and most computers are dependent on others, it is not enough to adjust one's own computer and rely on others to do the same. Inevitably, there will be those who will not respond. Is the problem not serious enough to contemplate, as the Singapore Government are doing, the introduction of statutory guidelines for businesses to follow?"

According to Atkinson, much had happened in the months since he first warned the Prime Minister of the problem in the

House of Commons the previous December (1995). He believed the government was taking some action regarding the computer systems for which they are responsible, and were alerting others of the need to do the same.

However, this was not enough. Atkinson's vision of the problem was the equivalent of a computer-apocalypse: "The century date change should be treated as the most devastating virus ever to affect our information technology system," he said. "The message from the debate must be clear. This is urgent. The majority of computer systems will fail if action is not taken, and the majority of companies are not aware of the problems they face.

"There are fewer than 850 working days left in which to take action. If action is not taken, companies will face enormous difficulties. This is one of the greatest challenges facing business management today. I look forward to my hon. Friend's response to a crisis that will face our national daily life in less than four years' time."

It was a ground-breaking speech. Although it only lasted 15 minutes it was the first time the mother of Parliaments had been warned in such stark terms. Ian Taylor, the government minister for science and technology who was responding to Atkinson's speech, stood up and took a deep breath. He welcomed what Atkinson's comments and said he was joining him in "raising the alarm". He thanked Atkinson for raising "this important issue" in the House, for pursuing it through questions and for discussing it with the minister.

"I openly admit he has informed my views on the subject," the minister said. "I have had the opportunity to discuss this with many people in the industry. This is a timely and necessary debate. It is surprising that a relatively simple issue can have such serious implications."

It was proof Whitehall was indeed waking up to the issue. Government ministers are loath to use phrases such as 'serious implications' without good cause. Taylor quoted a previous written answer he had given in the House of Commons: "The longer it is left, the higher the likely cost of remedial work. I am urging all chief executives to discover now for themselves the extent of the problem in their companies." *

*Official report, 8 May 1996; Vol. 277, c.152.

He pointed out that being aware of the problem and doing something about it were not the same thing. The survey, referred to with some concern by Atkinson, was conducted with the Central Computer and Telecommunications Agency (CCTA). It showed awareness of the problem was higher than 90 per cent, but action plans "had not been put into place". "That is the key point, and it is why I am so concerned about this issue."

Atkinson, said Taylor, had made some telling points about how computer systems could go wrong: "Pensioners and others could lose their pensions and entitlements - or certainly not be paid them; centenarians could appear on primary school intake lists; all military and aeronautical equipment could be simultaneously scheduled for maintenance; thousands of legal actions could be struck out; student loan repayments could be scheduled as overdue; and 100 years of interest could be added to credit card balances. With masterly understatement, the minister noted: "These things will not be particularly welcome".

He had more horror stories: "Data could be sorted in the incorrect order. For example, the years 2000 and 2001 could be sorted ahead of 1997 and 1998, which could affect hospital waiting lists. In addition, housing allocation priorities could be wrongly assigned." According to the minister there could be supply chain difficulties with errors being propagated through interconnected systems. "In other words," said Taylor, "it is vital that companies in supply chains take a mutual interest in attempting to eradicate the problem, to avoid a contagious disease."

A contagious disease? If only there had been more politicians present to hear the dire warning. Taylor said: "How long would companies survive if their customers could not pay their bills because their information system is not working. Non-conventional information technology systems could also fail: process control; access systems, such as swipe cards which would appear to be outside the period of validity; air-conditioning systems that are pre-programmed; weapons systems programs using two-digit dates embedded in out-of-production chips will have a particular problem; and safety-critical installations in nuclear power plants and in air traffic control.

"I have raised these points not to create a panic - I remind everyone that we are currently in 1996, so we have a while to go before the year 2000 - but to alert people to the fact that action taken now is absolutely vital, because there not be the opportunity to take action properly as the year 2000 approaches. I believe that some problems may emerge before the year 2000, which is why I am urging that audits are carried out into systems in various companies."

Taylor said huge resources will be needed to fix the problem: "For example, for some of the older systems the COBOL-trained staff could become scarce and perhaps prohibitively expensive. Organisations may find that they no longer have the people or skills used at the time that their systems were built. The criticality of the problem is its scale: the billions of lines of code to search, the fact that the deadline is immovable - we know that it will occur after midnight in the year 1999 - and the complexity and interdependency of the systems involved."

The minister said that suppliers of 'non-compliant' software must be checked out to establish whether they are prepared to fix the systems they installed or whether they intend to "walk away from the problem".

He added "Some say 50 per cent of information technology budgets will be spent on this problem, and therefore money might not be spent on more constructive developments... There are estimates that, if the current rate of progress is maintained, at least half of companies will not achieve compliance by the year 2000, which will be an appalling tragedy for those companies, and, because they are interconnected, for many others which have tried to be compliant. Obviously, some companies will go out of business..."

He listed some of the computer operating systems which need to be checked: IBM, MVS and UNIX, ICL, VME, Digital VMS, DOS, Windows and application software. It showed some civil servants had been doing their homework.

"Let me say a few words about action," said Taylor. "The CCTA has written to all government departments, alerting them and requesting details of the remedial action being undertaken... all new information technology procurements in Government and let through the CCTA must be millennium-compliant.

"Our systems in the Department of Trade and Industry are being reviewed. We have appointed consultants to plan a programme of work to make necessary changes to all systems to make them compliant by the year 2000; they will also work with our suppliers." He said the government had established a departmental management group which had discovered that at least one of the main systems at the DTI (the Department for Trade and Industry) used a four-digit year and should therefore be safe from catastrophe. "But," said Taylor, "I repeat that our suppliers may have systems that are not compliant so we have a considerable issue to resolve."

Taylor said he had urged all private sector chief executives not to leave the matter to their information technology managers. "It must be dealt with at the top," said the minister. "Chief executives of all companies of every size should conduct a demonstration of their computer system," and, even if they appear to have no problems, "which I would find surprising", they must ensure their suppliers and others who access their computing software do not have any either.

"The situation must be managed, and the sooner the better," he said. Victims of the millennium bomb were on their own; the Government could not do it for them. "It is no use companies coming to us in 1999 and saying, 'The Government have not fixed it'. The Government did not install the computer software. Failure to deal with the problem could lead to commercial collapse. I put it bluntly because I want to get the message across."

The Minister said he had written to the Bank of England, the Confederation of British Industry, the Institute of Directors, and a whole host of good and worthy trade organisations to publicise the problem. Meanwhile, the Computer Services and Software Association (CSSA), the leading trade association for the information sector, was working with the DTI to form a taskforce of users, suppliers and consultants. "There is no point in only the software suppliers looking at the problem; users must be involved in the task force as well."

The DTI would publicise the growing body of help and information through an Internet site on the World Wide Web, and through business links and Government offices, while the CSSA would operate a similar site and a business inquiry service to put inquirers in touch with firms specialising in solving the problem. Taylor said databases of millennium-compliant software are being compiled and updated, and conferences, seminars and workshops will be held.

Taylor was also tackling the global implications: "We shall raise the matter with the European Commission, and we are considering what international organisation is best able to tackle the problem - whether it is the Organisation for Economic Co-operation and Development or the World Trade Organisation," he said, promising bilateral talks with the American government. "Advances in technology are occurring so quickly that the problem may be resolved between now and 2000.

"New creative software packages may be designed that attack the problem at source. I am not overly optimistic, as many old systems must be dealt with. Nevertheless, I do not deny that there is a commercial incentive for someone to come forward with software that deals with the virus. We should be optimistic in that regard, bearing in that computer power doubles every 14 months for the same price, the use of the Internet doubles every nine months and that we are seeing an explosion in information technology around the world. It is inconceivable that anyone who is involved in the industry, be it as a supplier, hardware manufacturer, software creator or as a user, would wish to see the problem occur in 2000 and destroy so much creative effort and excellent information technology work."

With that final rallying cry, the minister resumed his seat. His speech was remarkable in its frankness and in the detail of its analysis but Taylor knew he was not the only senior politician getting worried. A few weeks earlier the United States Congress had aired concerns about the millennium bomb problem, although its style was somewhat different. In April 1996 experts testified before a Congressional subcommittee on government management, information and technology and the warnings in America were as stark as those delivered in the mother of Parliaments.

Peter de Jager, a computer consultant and millennium bomb expert with an international reputation was blunt: "I will leave you to contemplate what happens to the world-wide economy if businesses lose the ability to do business," he said. "We have no time for unjustified optimism. Nor have we time for cautious optimism. We have time only for a highly accelerated sense of urgency, a meagre allotment of time rapidly slipping away."

De Jager was probably the first to warn North America of the potential crisis and he launched into his speech by saying that computer practitioners are the most optimistic people in the world and that, despite all evidence to the contrary, they believe the next program they create will finally be 'bug free'. "We believe the bug we just found is the last one," said de Jager. "We believe the next release of a software product will solve all the errors in the prior release and introduce no new ones. Sadly, these beliefs are totally without foundation. Our clients know this.

He was not the only person to deliver testimony to the Congressional subcommittee. It heard from several experts about the possible impact of the millennium date change problem. With some it was necessary to read between the lines: experts reprogramming the New York Stock Exchange's computers gave the impression everything was progressing happily but when cross-examined they admitted they were having problems with "testing and implementation". Republican Stephen Horn, the subcommittee chairman and a former college professor later commented: "If you wait until 1998 to do the job, there won't be the resources available; they will already be gobbled up by some other group, private or public at all levels of government, and we're going to get down to a crunch. We're trying to sensitise the executive branch," he said.

Across the border in Canada, the federal government believes the Year 2000 problem poses significant dangers. "A central Year 2000 project Office has been established within the Treasury Board Secretariat to ensure that Departments address the problem and share their findings," said P M McLellan, the Assistant Deputy Minister for the Government Telecommunications and Informatics Services (TIS). McLellan said the cost of finding a fix for TIS alone was conservatively estimated at $25 million.

The raising of the issue on Capitol Hill and in the Houses of Parliament in such stark terms prompted national newspapers and the international media to latch on the story. Could it really happen, asked the journalists, that there would be no money available from banks, no food distribution and trains and buses would not run?

The issue was also taken up by Britain's opposition Labour Party which hinted it may have to review its economic plans to take account of the enormous bill for remedial action. "If it really is going to cost us £5 billion then we would need to go back to the books and work out how we are going to pay for it," said one senior party official. "It is an astronomical sum that cannot be magically produced or taken from the budget for the health service or social security. This is not something any government in the world has properly budgeted for."

It is a signal that once such realities sink in, politicians will seek to make political capital. It is a beguiling idea, for those who jump on the bandwagon can be winners both ways. If they adopt a doom and gloom stance and make dire predictions of the collapse of western economies, and then nothing drastic happens, they can claim that their warnings were heeded. If nobody listens to their warnings and there is a millennium meltdown, they can claim they 'told us so'. But no-one will forgive those who choose to ignore the problem in the hope it will solve itself.

Chapter Four

FIGHTING A MILITARY CAMPAIGN

"Unless action is taken by the Ministry of Defence and the Pentagon we will inevitably see their entire computer systems shutting down; their computers could crash and there will be chaos." This is the blunt warning to the military from Professor Keith Bennett, head of the computer science unit at Durham University and one of few academics to study the potential impact of the millennium problem. The US Department of Defense and the British Ministry of Defence are already admitting they face a tougher task than industry because almost every computer system they use is at risk.

In the 1980s, a film called 'Wargames' vividly illustrated the power of modern military computers. The movie featured a young computer whizkid who 'hacked' his way into one of the most sensitive American military machines from the comfort of his bedroom. Matthew Broderick, the star, did it to impress girls, not the Soviet KGB, but the FBI dragged him off for interrogation when the defence computer started to malfunction. After Broderick hacked into the computer it started to play out a 'game' during which it went onto a war-footing and tried to launch nuclear missiles at the Soviets. The 'game' only stopped when the heroes persuaded the computer to play tic-tac-toe (noughts & crosses).

Banal as it may sound, the film depicted the military's reliance on automated computer systems including those commanding conventional and nuclear weapons. It is no fiction to say that the defence of many Western nations is now under the control of computers. Hollywood was pointing to the huge potential for disaster when responsibility is transferred from humans to computerised technology.

The "MoD is aware of the potential dangers caused by the so-called 'millennium bomb' across all our support, operational and embedded systems," said John Trebble, the Ministry of Defence's national Year 2000 Programme Manager. "The scale of the total problem is akin to mounting a major combined military exercise for the next three years. Within the support area alone we have over 500 major systems covering finance, human resources and logistics. All systems have to be checked for Year 2000 compliance to ensure that they continue to function correctly in the new millennium, and interoperability between these and other systems is not jeopardised."

Dealing with the problem, admits the MoD, will cost at least £100 million over the next few years.According to Trebble, a number of systems have already experienced problems, mainly in the support areas. Trebble gives the example of pay and pension systems, where the extensive use of forward date calculations is made, as well as personnel systems where a considerable degree of forward planning occurs in managing servicemen's careers. But what about the more serious aspects of the glitch in military equipment, such as communications? Trebble is unequivocal: "On the operational side, messaging systems and space satellite communication systems are two areas where date recording and

A CRAY-2 supercomputer being installed for NASA in 1985. It was to be used for flight simulation work and was three times faster than its predecessor. Sales of CRAY computers to many countries were banned because their phenomenal speed and power could be used to design nuclear weapons.

calculations are made which may be susceptible to Year 2000 related problems." According to other experts, the millennium bugs could shut-down satellites, destroying international phone connections, and can only be fixed if the satellites are physically retrieved and modified.

But even with this high level of concern a number of military personnel - even those who use computer equipment every day of their working lives - profess complete ignorance of the millennium bomb. However the Ministry of Defence claim much work has been done to identify potential problem areas and raise awareness: "A Defence Council Instruction was issued on 5th July [1996] to warn all MoD personnel of this problem and give general advice and points of contact," Trebble said. He clearly believed the MoD was on top of it, and noted the Ministry was preparing a policy statement and guide which "mandate an impact assessment" for ALL (MoD's emphasis) information technology systems, including weapons systems.

Trebble added: "An outline methodology is provided and a help desk facility is being established to co-ordinate activity across the whole of MoD. An MoD Year 2000 Steering Committee has been established and will hold its third meeting in early October 1996 to monitor progress against the agreed action plan." A programme to raise awareness of the issue amongst senior management was also being prepared."

The MoD admitted that the figure of £100 million over the next three years was "very much an initial assessment". Full budgetary estimates for the cost of making systems 'millennium friendly' would not be available until mid-1997 after impact assessments had been processed and decisions made on prioritisation.

On the question of whether weapons systems will be crippled, Trebble took a distinctly up-beat view of the problem in Britain: "It is likely that very few, if any, weapons systems will be affected. However, all such systems must be investigated, and a methodology is being developed to ensure that this task is carried out thoroughly. All major systems will be fixed or replaced, but it is inevitable that some small PC-based systems may be overlooked.

"A contingency plan will be developed to ensure that any small system that is missed can be assessed and dealt with. The reliance on computer-based technology within MoD for support, operational and embedded systems is such that problems caused by the Year 2000 date change must not be allowed to impact on the operational effectiveness of the business of MoD. This is reflected in the programme management put in place, and the projects to be run by systems managers to identify and correct any problems." As the MoD so candidly admits, the scale of the bug is huge, but whether it can fix the problem in time remains to be seen. So far it has established an internal help-desk, and compiled a four-point plan to deal with the problem, which starts with a survey of its major computer systems, then continues with a huge awareness project to explain the glitch to senior officers, officials and servicemen and women.

However, according to several serving and retired British military computer programmers we have contacted, the MoD might actually be under-estimating the scale of the problem, both in operational systems (such as missile control computers) and support systems (the computers which process payments, pensions and order supplies – all vital for keeping the military working).

"Our computers are crashing all the time," said one Naval officer who asked to remain anonymous because she still works in the support side of the armed services. "We are lumbered with outdated, under-powered computer equipment that has been tinkered with over the years until they have become machines which their original manufacturers would barely recognise." Another computer expert we contacted worked at a senior level within the military, in charge of a unit which actually created programmes to run military equipment, such as a fighter aircraft or an advanced tank. He is still bound by the Official Secrets Act, and asked to remain anonymous. "When I was working for the MoD a number of years ago I made sure that it was common practice to put a four-digit date code in all the computers and programmes my team was working on because of my concerns that the new millennium was not as far in the distance as some of my peers seemed to think," he said.

" It seemed obvious to me that we might be still using the same programs – or a modified version of them – at the end of the 1990s. I've only just discovered that some of the programs I created for the military have since been replaced by more modern programs which were supposed to be the best the MoD could get, but I've also discovered that while the old programs were 'millennium-friendly', the new ones aren't! Those missing dates could cause computers to crash."

It seems unlikely the British armed forces are in a stronger position to deal with the problem than the Americans, and the picture emerging in Washington is gloomy. The Department of Defense, with its headquarters at the Pentagon, is the largest single user of computers in the world, and much of its technology is the most expensive money can buy. In the words of Emmett Paige, the American Assistant Secretary of Defense in charge of command, control, communications and intelligence, his forces are totally "dependent" on them.

Indeed computers are becoming weapon systems in their own right. The US Department of Defense has recently launched a new initiative on what it calls information warfare. Official reports speak of bombarding enemies with 'information munitions' or black propaganda while America protects itself with a 'bodyguard of lies', yet more misinformation.

The Internet is one medium through which this computerised war will be fought. But before such novel uses of the computer can be exploited the world's military machines must struggle to defuse the self-inflicted information munitions in its own Trojan horse - the millennium bomb. The US Airforce described it as "one heart-stopper of a problem".

The CIA started work on fixing its own computers three years ago. "We are aware of the millennium problem, and we are dealing with it," said sources within the Agency. "We use the very latest computer technology. This is a world-wide problem, and we are no different to anyone else". Certainly no different to the American Department of Defense, where early estimates of the size of the problem are truly astonishing: at least 358 million lines of code may need to be checked for bugs.

Paige has highlighted the possible effects on costly military hardware. He described the glitch as a 'serious problem' which the Pentagon is treating 'much as we would a computer virus'. In an address to a Congressional hearing on April 16th 1996, he said:

Emmett Paige, America's Assistant Secretary of Defense for Command, Communications and Intelligence. He told Congress some of his country's weapon systems could fail because of the Year-2000 problem.

"The impact of taking no action on the Year 2000 problem is that we risk the high probability of severely hampering, in some cases, many defense activities. Some of those activities will involve military operations. Does this place some of these operations at risk? I believe that it does."

"The Department of Defense has some relatively unique Year 2000 problems," said Paige. "Our software inventory includes software written in computer languages, such as Jovial, that are not widely used elsewhere. This is a legacy of past policies that permitted the proliferation of different computer languages and dialects." Paige said the Pentagon is working "aggressively" towards correcting the language problem. "This means we will need a wider array of software tools to help reduce the time to find and fix Year 2000 problems, and to validate the solutions through testing. Commercial off-the-shelf software tools are available only for some of the more commonly used computer programming languages, such as COBOL, C, and, of course, Ada. For many computer languages, no commercial tools are available."

The implications of Paige's last sentence are serious. Some of the military's computer languages are only understood by a handful of experts and it is clear the military has left it perilously late to start investigating their computers. There are no special technological 'silver bullets' they can use to change all their computers and much of the checking and changing will have to be done laboriously by hand in the months and weeks left before the end of the century.

So what will this cure cost? Mitre Corp., a company in Bedford, Massachusetts, has conducted an investigation of the extent of the problem for the Pentagon, and has concluded the Department of Defence will need to spend between $0.75 and $8.52 per line of code to fix its Year 2000 glitch. Rewriting software could cost more than $1 billion, but that is only part of the problem: "We may find the Year 2000 date problem in computer chips used only by the Department of Defense," warned the Assistant Secretary of State. "Those chips may no longer be in production. Some of these chips are [made] because of special military requirements, such as in a missile." Paige admitted that this ludicrous situation stems from previous military policy that specified the use of unique custom-made chips not used by anyone else, rather than cheaper commercially available chips.

But why do the military need such costly computer equipment in the first place? Part of the expense is due to the unique demands they make on their technology: on-board missile computers must be capable of withstanding the pressures of travelling faster than the speed of sound and then 'punching' through concrete or armour plating before exploding and destroying their target, be it an enemy bunker in southern Baghdad or a tank on the plains of Russia.

The chips are everywhere. Naval computers operate below the waves in torpedoes and ICBM's (inter-continental ballistic missiles) on submarines. In the air, computers remove much of the controls from pilots of the latest bombers. Many fighter aircraft, such as the American F-15 or British Jaguar, are so complicated that nearly all the work and decisions are taken by computers which locate targets, fix them in their memories and choose whether guns or missiles are the best weapon with which to attack. Millennium bugs in the military are often built into parts of the computers which cannot be easily replaced.

In his testimony to Congress, Paige noted how American society (just like every other industrialised nation) has become dependent on computers, and his department reflects that. "We have fundamentally restructured our institutions over many years to exploit computing and telecommunications technologies. We are dependent on our computer and telecommunications systems." Paige said if a particular computer system failed, the military have generally learned how to work around an individual failure: "However, if a problem that happens to be common in most of our systems, were to cause failures in all of those systems at the same instant, the consequences might be catastrophic. The Year 2000 problem has these characteristics."

He went on to describe some of the difficulties this might cause at the start of a new millennium: "If our personnel and payroll systems process dates incorrectly, current employees, members of the armed services, and our 'annuitants' cannot be properly paid. If our logistics and transportation systems process dates incorrectly, people and equipment cannot be delivered to the correct place at the correct time. This, of course, could have catastrophic consequences should it happen during a time when our fighting forces are being called upon to react to national security crisis or lend emergency assistance. Some of our weapons systems would not function properly. Our databases would be greatly corrupted."

Members of the Congressional subcommittee listened in astonishment as Paige went on: "Inaction is simply unacceptable, co-ordinated and collaborative action is imperative. Fortunately, weapons systems are, for the most part, much less date-intensive than most business information systems so there are fewer Year 2000 fixes which need to be made in them. Nevertheless, we still have to check all weapons systems for the Year 2000 problem. When we are dealing with weapons and their delivery systems, we must leave nothing to chance." They certainly cannot because nobody really knows exactly what commands have been left behind from the darkest days of the Cold War. This was the era when doomsday theorists programmed last ditch instructions into computers enabling missiles to attack the enemy without a full set of orders from human military controllers if the West was swamped by a surprise nuclear or conventional attack from Eastern bloc nations.

Paige said the limited amount of time left to solve the problem is already causing problems for the Pentagon. He told the Congressional committee that once it was identified within a system, the Year 2000 problem is usually 'trivial' to solve. It is, however, an "enormous" management problem.

"The Department has an inventory of thousands of systems and hundreds of millions of lines of computer code. Finding, fixing, and testing date-related processing in our systems will require significant resources, resources that generally have not been planned or programmed for this purpose. No politician likes to admit that more money will be needed to solve a problem, but Paige was adamant: "We believe we will have to expend significant funds to complete the task. We are working diligently to quickly refine our assessments across the Department. However, it is becoming clear that trade-offs will be required."

The cost of curing the computers will be so large, said Paige, that many other initiatives may need to be delayed. "With resources for the Federal government becoming increasingly scarce, DoD will continue to examine its priorities carefully when considering funding for information technology investments, including those for the services and defense Agencies to fix or remedy the Year 2000 problem. We must work within the constraints of overall budget realities."

Two months after Paige's Congressional testimony, a dramatic order came from the office of the US Secretary of Defense to the army, navy and airforce - every defence establishment. It instructed them to check all their computer systems: "to ensure weapon, command and control, and information system proponents, sponsors, designers, developers, maintainers and users are aware of potential software, firmware and hardware failures associated with the arrival of the year 2000... corrective actions, if not currently underway, should start now."

In June 1996, Paige directed the military services and defence agencies to stop working on every current contract until they have assurances in writing that new computers will be millennium-friendly. He has also warned individual departments they will be financially responsible for fixing their own computers.

According to the Pentagon, the worst case scenario resulting from the millennium bomb is that weaponry could be triggered and missiles fired. A less disastrous scenario is that hundred of thousands of military personnel may not get their pay cheques, ammunition or food. In between there are a host of possibilities for millennium meltdown, ranging from the loss of ability for the military to navigate ships or track aircraft, to a black comedy of administrative and logistic administration errors.

MILITARY and civil aircraft face common millennium problems. When aviation computers malfunction or breakdown they can cause accidents, but such incidents are normally isolated, not the multiple failures that could be triggered by the century date change. The concerns about aviation computers and the millennium bomb are wide-ranging and start with worries that control

> The millennium problem is not the only computer threat troubling the military. The Department of Defense has admitted it is at risk from what has been described as a 'Pearl Harbour' onslaught from cyberspace. In July 1996 the Clinton government warned of a potential catastrophic 'cyber attack' on networks by terrorists or blackmailers, and Clinton himself ordered an independent Presidential commission to investigate the risks both to defence systems and more fundamental areas such as telephone systems, financial services, medical records, power grids, and gas and water supplies.
>
> According to Jamie Gorelick, Deputy Attorney-General, a joint public and private effort was needed to thwart the threat. "What we need is the equivalent of the Manhattan Project," said Gorelick, in a reference to the code name of the project that developed atomic weapons during the Second World War. "It is that level of urgency. It is our clear view that a cyber threat can disrupt the provision of services, can disrupt our society, disable our society, even more so than can a well-placed bomb." Gorelick believes an attack will come sooner rather than later.
>
> John Deutch, the director of the CIA, described the threat of a cyber attack as the second biggest security headache facing the US.

maintenance programmes will automatically shut-down if they are not properly serviced. At the simplest level, machines might think parts have not been maintained for 99 years after January 1st 2000 and ground planes in which they are installed. Onboard computers could malfunction when a plane is in flight. Most systems are supposedly fail-safe so that a pilot could take over in an emergency, yet there are still worries about safety.

Several sources within the international airline industry disclosed that at least three major airlines have apparently been advised by their most senior computer experts not to fly their planes over the weekend on which the start of the next millennium will fall. Other experts have warned that some commercial air-traffic control radar systems use computer chips which recognise and interpret the date '00' as a so-called 'interrupt' which can cause radar to stop working or malfunction.

"We have been aware of the millennium problem since 1987 when we introduced a new computer database," said Peter Blundell, the data design manager for British Airways and the company's Year 2000 co-ordinator. "When we brought in the new computer we saw it had a problem with the Year 2000 and we suddenly realised the dangers. The implications of the problem for firms are, in general, very serious.

"We have a team working to solve the problems and we should have altered all the dates in our computers by the end of 1998. This is one project where we cannot change the end-date but because we started working on it quite a few years ago it is costing significantly less than it will for other firms."

BA was one of the first companies in Europe to establish a unit to work on the millennium bomb, and will have to re-program at least 400 computer systems to guarantee its computers will continue to operate normally. The firm has more than 15,000 personal computers in 750 locations world-wide. When the taskforce was established, its head confirmed that all ticket booking, payroll, check-in and catering systems would be affected by the millennium bomb. Unless rectified, a customer trying to book a flight on

January 1st, 2000, would learn from the reservation system there were no flights available. "Before we set up the taskforce, everyone joked there was going to be a problem but they wouldn't be around to deal with it and it would be somebody else's headache," said Terry Worth, in charge of 'service recovery' for BA, a computer-troubleshooter dealing with crashes and glitches. Worth was involved in establishing the taskforce and was one of a small team which wrote a report about the Year 2000 problem and gave it to the director of information technology and other management.

The report warned that the firm was running out of time to fix the bugs: "We were a little bit dramatic to grab their attention," said Worth. "We had to tell them it was going to affect almost every aspect of our business. We have done a thorough review and, although it is a trivial problem, the fact that it is in so many of our programmes means it is not easy to track everything down. The worry in my mind at the time was that people could not realise the immediacy of the problem."

Worth acknowledged managing directors might be annoyed at spending money on curing a problem they cannot understand and which will not actually advance the firm forward. "But it will mean the company survives the year 2000," he said.

BA's staff are also asking questions as they realise the dangers. "With the onset of January 1, 2000, the 2000 will be read by computer systems as 00, potentially causing a complete system failure or producing incorrect calculations in time-sensitive programmes," wrote R. Sherrard, who works in Production Control at Heathrow, in a recent edition of the internal company newspaper. "At risk are all mainframe systems, PC's, networks and peripherals. The millennium problem has the potential not only to severely disrupt businesses, but whole economies."

Sherrard said he had conducted a test on his computers to see whether the Year 2000 would affect the machines, and was less than happy with what he found. "Are we aware of this problem and if so, what steps are being taken to fix or upgrade our software?" he asked. Peter Blundell responded with some reassurance. He said BA was taking the opportunity to replace some computer systems in the small number of cases where the machines need costly changes, where the supplier has gone out of business or is "unwilling to change old systems".

Many airlines around the world are only just realising how all-pervasive the date problem is in their computers and are establishing specialist teams of experts to fix the glitch. Industry sources estimate more than one hundred major airlines face the same millennium problems as British Airways but while BA has been working on its software for years and will not finish for another two years, many of the others have not yet started.

Unfortunately, airline systems are only part of the equation. Air traffic controllers rely upon highly computerised systems to locate, track, communicate with and direct both incoming and outbound aircraft in the crowded skies. The volume of information which computers can hold, the rate at which they can process the information and transfer it onto computer screens for the pilots and controllers far outstrips the ability of the unassisted human mind. It is just not possible to keep today's volumes of aviation in the sky with safe vertical and horizontal distances between planes without computerisation.

On several occasions in recent years, air traffic systems have 'gone down' and forced their controllers to rush for pen and paper. Pilots in the sky have had to revert to emergency visual flight procedures and take their own avoiding action based on what they can physically see from the cockpit. Disasters have been only been avoided because the incidents have been short-lived and isolated. A more widespread or long lasting bug in air traffic control computers could put all aircraft on the ground. The US Federal Aviation Authority, British Civil Aviation Authority and other air traffic control computers world-wide have experienced these frightening computer 'hiccups' several times.

Aircraft themselves are also reliant on computers controlling both flight operations and navigation. In Europe's airbus, operations are almost completely 'fly-by-wire'. Many modern passenger aircraft know where they are because of information fed to on-board computers linked to an inertial navigation system (INS) and global positioning system (GPS). INS depends on accurate input of information derived from computers. The GPS system makes use of a network of satellites in low earth orbit (LEO). These transmit signals to a receiver on board, for example, an aircraft. By comparing signals from a number of GPS satellites, the exact position of the plane can be calculated. But the system is dependent on computer clocks and the timing difference between signals.

GPS can be compared to a giant electronic sextant. In star navigation, an almanac or tables record the pre-calculated positions of various stars at a certain date and time. Geometry then allows the observer to determine his position on the surface of the earth relative to the heavenly bodies.

In the GPS system the stars are a constellation of satellites whose position is known at any fraction of a second in time. The system software keeps its own electronic almanac and contact with these electronic 'stars' is established not by eyesight in the visible spectrum but by radio waves. The satellites are equipped with a software program which allows them to send out a transmission which effectively says: "I am here, this is my ID, and this is the time and date at which I am sending out this signal." It takes a certain amount of time for that signal pulse to be received as the radio waves travel though space.

The GPS receiver is able to calculate from the timing difference between the stated transmission time and the received time how far it is from that satellite. It receives this information from several such satellites and calculates its position by triangulation, so the more satellites it is tuned to the greater the accuracy and the less room for doubt.

The system has both civil and military application and the US Department of Defense and its allies have blocked the more accurate equipment being made available for civil applications, apparently because of concerns that terrorists or renegade states would use it to create accurate missile tracking systems.

During the Gulf War, allied forces were able to establish the position of targets and their own troop emplacements to within just a few metres. The military divided Kuwait and Iraq up into highly calibrated grids along which missiles, troops and aircraft could fly to their targets. Similar reliance is placed on GPS by the aviation industry and by the world's shipping fleets. A number of haulage firms and bus companies now track their passenger or freight transport vehicles by GPS as a means of timing schedules.

The virtue is that it is accurate and works in fog and darkness but it may not work in 1999 because of clock problems. According Joe Gwinn, an acknowledged expert on the systems, unmodified GPS equipment will fail at midnight on 21st August 1999. The GPS date counters were started at midnight on 5th-6th January 1980 and the code has a 1024 week cycle. Since years have 52 weeks, the unit has an effective timespan of 19.7 years.

According to Gwinn, the computers have no means of knowing the second cycle has begun after 22 August 1999. The opinion of one manufacturer is that every GPS unit they have manufactured would have to come back for repair under warranty. The software in all older units will have to be replaced. In some cases the relevant chip that needs changing is plugged-in, and in other cases it is soldered.

New software would log each 1024 week cycle and recognise the second roll-over date which comes another 19.7 years later in 2019 AD. It is not an insoluble technical problem but millions of units will have to be recalled. Unless this starts early, there will be a massive logistical jam. Certainly many millions of dollars need to be spent to make systems function beyond August 1999, and that presumes the satellites on which GPS depends are not infected with the Year 2000 problem.

Yet military spy satellites and normal commercial satellites could malfunction. Professor Keith Bennett, head of the Computer Science Unit at Durham University, said: "Some of the code can be 'upline loaded' straight into the satellite, but some of the core stuff could well be built in; often parts of the satellite manipulating time and dates are 'core' and therefore not accessible without retrieval."

Many international phone links routed through geo-stationary satellites will be wiped-out unless action is taken, according to Bennett. He said the potential nuclear and defence implications are the most fascinating and worrying of all. "Military, process control and nuclear all tend to have systems which are very long-lived and, if anything, these are the systems for which money was tight when they were first written and they went for two-digit dates," said Bennett.

Other academics share his concerns, particularly about the effects on computers in crucial areas such as nuclear power stations and nuclear defence systems. Professor Philip Wadler from the Department of Computing Science at Glasgow University believes that accidents in the past show that it is very difficult to spot even minor errors in computers systems. Wadler's university describes him as an expert on safety critical computing systems, but Wadler, who works on the design of computer languages, modestly says it is an area he is particularly interested in. "To get high performance, military airplanes - especially fighters, are inherently unstable. Computers keep them stable. If the computer crashes then the plane crashes, and that has happened. The date problem could cause these system failures," said Wadler, who grew up in American's Silicon Valley but went to Glasgow nine years ago because the university is one of the leading centres in the world for his area of study. "It is hard to think of a safety critical system that doesn't use the time and date." Indeed, the whole fabric of society could be affected.

Chapter Five

DISTRESS IN THE CITY

The image is of a stock market drowning in paper and panic. The computer programs that once ran sophisticated operations buying and selling shares around the globe lie obsolete, their plugs ripped out by frantic traders who could not prevent them selling shares when they were switched on during the first Monday morning of the next millennium...it is a nightmare that will keep many City computer experts awake at night over the next few years as they ponder what could happen if they fail to modify hundreds of thousands of computers which are absolutely crucial to the success or collapse or our economies. At the Stock Exchange in London, one of the largest and most important in the world, experts appear aware of the millennium bomb but refuse to discuss it openly for fear of damaging "investor confidence".

Their concern is understandable. The finance and banking sector could suffer more than most when millennium bugs start to wreak havoc. The sector is highly dependent on computers and those institutions that fail to deal with the problem in time will have few excuses for their shareholders. They have known about the possible impact of the millennium bomb for as least as long as the computer companies, and some were already experiencing problems with the Year 2000 up to 30 years ago.

Banks and insurance companies are reluctant to discuss problems they suffered in previous decades but some horror stories have been revealed. An American insurance company in a mid-Western state spent more than $3 million on a new computer set-up in the early seventies which was supposed to make the firm's computerised operations even more efficient. Then it discovered it had to withdraw a popular retirement policy because it had an end-date in the next century and the system could not handle the data.

A British bank runs advertisements on television proclaiming its forward-thinking. It overlooks the time its computers crashed in the early 1980s when entered with details of a 20 year investment plan. Enquiries show it has only just started to take remedial action to cure the glitch. In 1993 an Australian insurance company's information processing system crashed while working on a seven year policy because the programme could not comprehend the year 2000. The thankless programmer punching keys then decided to continue, substituting an end date of 1999 so that the risk and income were now spread over six years as opposed to seven. Inside the machine, the mathematics failed. Experts eventually managed to save the system, but not before prospective clients had their incomes overstated by millions of dollars.

Dozens of other failures remain secret but within the industry they provide a lesson that this is a problem to be tackled not shelved. Many Wall Street firms are being spurred on to take action by the worry that the regulatory authorities may impose deadlines by which all computers must be millennium-friendly. The Securities and Exchange Commission is particularly concerned and has said it will be questioning firms about the bug in future examinations of registered brokers, dealers, investment advisers and investment companies. "It is imperative that the securities and investment industries take action to protect their systems from these problems," wrote Lori Richards, the director of the SEC's inspection office, in a letter leaked in June 1996. "Our examiners will be asking each firm to ensure that appropriate modifications to software are made." Richards added: "We want to make sure that all firms in the securities industry are aware of the issue...".

Recently a number of broking firms on Wall Street, the financial heart of New York, have been offered a free computer analysis of the problem by the firms which sold them their computers - many of which are said to be terrified by the prospect of litigation. Elsewhere in North America, the banking community is starting to take action after warnings from experts like David Reingold, the vice-president of Computer Horizons, who warned that most banks in New York cannot issue five-year certificates of deposit because computers cannot handle the data. KPMG Peat Marwick has established a global Year 2000 practice to help its banking customers modify codes in their huge mainframe computers.

"The problem is everywhere, especially in our industry where we are so date-related," David Icaino, a senior manager at the Bank of Boston, told the American Bankers' Association in May 1996. Bank of Boston will devote 100 man years, or 33 people working full time on the problem for at least three years to fix most of its computer programs.

Icaino admitted to the Association that his bank was initially sceptical of the damage that the Year 2000 could do to its computers, and only really started to accept the full implications after 1994. The bank had adopted the same type of approach to the problem as that used by hospital casualty doctors during major accidents where the worst injured are treated first. Programs dealing with customers, the American federal reserve and financial applications must be given emergency attention, otherwise the business would simply collapse, while programs that churn out internal data reports are way down the list of priorities.

Bank of Boston's IT department has uncovered some interesting anomalies during tests of its computers to check the extent of the glitch, according to the American Bankers' Association Journal. In the tests, IBM-type personal computers and Apple Macintosh machines behaved erratically when set to a date of February 1, 2000. The personal computers reset their dates to 1/2/100. The Macs appeared to accept the date change at first and then reset to their base years.

BankAmerica Corporation has admitted it holds 95 million lines of time-sensitive code that need to be - in the words of one expert - "tweaked". Howard Adams, a vice-president of the bank, based in San Francisco, told Computerworld in March 1996: "We have estimated that we are going to have to go through 2,700 lines of code an hour from now until January 1st 2000 to get through this. Even if you know what the problem is, where do you draw the resources to deal with it?" Another large bank, America's Banc One, have been working on defusing their own millennium bombs for the last four years and have replaced their two-digit date codes with four-digits.

But it is not just the 'big-boys' who are facing difficulties. Tom Wiles is the senior vice-president of West Plains Bank in Missouri, which has just $107 million in assets. He is one of the few heads of smaller companies to accept the effects of the millennium bug. "I never greatly worried about it. I knew my computer system would crash but I also assumed I'd be making a change before the Year 2000," he told the Banking Journal in May, 1996. Wiles changed most of his computers - 'upgraded' them to use the jargon of the industry - and says he will not suffer from the glitches that will affect his competitors. He just needs to replace some of the bank's spreadsheet programs, which he would probably have wanted to do anyway in the next few years, and his bank should be one of the few that are quite safe when the decade ends.

In Canada, The Laurentian Bank is also hoping it will solve its problems in time. The bank said it realised the extent of the Year 2000 problem during the first few months of 1994, largely because of glitches during the calculations of five-year mortgages. CGI Group, a consulting firm based in Montreal, were called in to find a solution, with the result that Laurentian is now spending millions of dollars and several years to modify its entire computer systems.

"This is not just a mainframe problem," said Ron O'Donoughue, the head of a team at the Royal Bank of Canada established to fix the Year 2000 problem. "It can affect anything with a microprocessor. That includes PC's, security systems, even some elevators. Everything affecting our banking applications must be changed over the next three years - mainframe, individual workstations, third-party software, electronic transactions and business forms - in more than 30 countries." The bank proclaims its forward-thinking: "The Royal Bank was one of the first companies in Canada to recognise Y2K [a common North American acronym for the problem] and is on schedule to have all of its 600 computer systems reprogrammed by the end of 1998. The cost of the project to the bank could reach $50 million, but that is considerably less than companies that were slower to get started." While most Canadian businesses are aware of the problem, only about 25 to 30 per cent are doing anything about it, according to the Royal Bank.

In the Caribbean, the Bank of Jamaica has been aware of the problem since 1987 and is keen to raise awareness to prevent its customers and corporate clients experiencing a collapse of their own computers. "It is envisaged that there will be a number of computer problems," said Michael Buckle, an assistant director in the Bank of Jamaica's Information Systems Department, which is currently examining all the bank's computers for glitches. In the southern hemisphere, Debbie Monigatti, the communications manager of the National Bank of New Zealand, has prepared a pamphlet for many of her bank's corporate clients warning them of the millennium bomb and the dangers of inaction.

IN BRITAIN meanwhile, the Bank of England, National Westminster and Midland Bank have joined various help-groups to discuss the millennium problem and seek solutions. Here too, there is a cloak of secrecy, for 'security reasons', and perhaps also because customers might be none too impressed by an institution which could not forsee the coming millennium. When talking on the record few bank officials admitted serious problems but, offered anonymity, they were more forthcoming: "We are looking at a cost of anything up to £50 million to resolve this ridiculous problem," said the Year 2000 programme manager for one of the largest British banks.

As already reported, Ian Taylor, the British minister for science and technology, has written to the Bank of England's deputy governor and heads of other major British financial institutions warning them of Year 2000 problems. The Bank of England produced a prepared statement which showed it had responded: "The Bank of England is assisting the Department of Trade and Industry in making companies aware of the problem, which certainly for some organisations will be very serious. Our own computers have already been attended to."

"Knowledge of this problem is high in the information technology world, but the financial community is relatively ignorant," said Graham Williams, the head of Coopers & Lybrand computer assurance services group, to Accountancy Age in early 1996. Williams believes that after 1st January 2000, date-dependent data will become 'meaningless'. "I have one large UK financial services client which estimates that the problem will take 100 man-years to correct," he told the magazine. "It is a potential Doomsday scenario. It may prove cheaper for some organisations to replace all their systems, rather than rewrite the programs. Rewriting could take too long, and the clock is ticking." Eagle Star, one of Britain's biggest insurance companies, appears to be taking William's advice. It is replacing many of its most important computer systems - at a cost of millions of pounds - rather than spending hundreds of man-years trying to make them millennium friendly.

IF BANKS are at risk, so are many more government departments. Governments are huge, lumbering machines, and their departments' penchant for bureaucracy and form-filling lent itself easily to computerisation in the last 30 years. Why just have several paper copies of a document or data when you can also store it on computer? Governments at both local and national level have embraced computer technology with a passion, and store massive quantities of data on their machines.

Unfortunately, governments never have enough money to spend on their own operation, and their parsimonious attitudes are reflected in the technology they are forced to use. Around the world, governments tend to hang onto their old computers as long as possible. They are the largest users of old main-frames that require constant maintenance, and it is these that are most at risk from the millennium bomb.

In Britain, the Department of Social Security's computer branch - the Information Technology Systems Agency (ITSA) - has been considering the problem since before June 1995. It is responsible for running all the department's machines, the country's biggest set-up, holding social security data on millions of citizens. "We are working on the computers to check the extent of the problem after the Year 2000," said senior official Gerry Mulrooney. "The key benefit delivery systems and some other systems will need to have some work done to them."

Mulrooney said he is confident that key benefits will not fail and will still be paid. However, he admitted there was deep concern within ITSA about the effects of the Millennium Bomb, and officials are already discussing the possibility of resorting to litigation to pay for computer changes. "We are looking at going back to the suppliers to sort it out," admits Mulrooney. "We are very nearly, if not totally 100 per cent reliant on computers to operate. People do not seem to have given the millennium bug enough thought and it is an issue that must be addressed."

That criticism has been levelled at another big user of computers in Britain, the Inland Revenue. As one of the Government's main tax-raising authorities it is heavily reliant on data processing. Their computer officials said only that the cost of making the changes will be found from the overall IT budget; there was no clear message as to whether it would make those changes on time.

If British government departments listen to their own advisors, they would realise they have no grounds for complacency. The Central Communications and Telecommunications Agency (CCTA) is the chief advisor to government on the millennium bomb, and Bob Assirati, chief executive, has given vociferous warnings of the dangers of inaction. "If we ignore this problem it could be a question of survival for many businesses," he said.

Michael Heseltine, Britain's Deputy Prime Minister, is 'very concerned' about the millennium problem and his Government is backing a number of initiatives to find solutions.

The CCTA has a vital role to play in raising awareness of the problem through its central function as the main computer advisers to government departments and other large public bodies. Robin Guenier, a lawyer and the CCTA's former chief executive, travelled to America to learn more about the glitch before briefing Michael Heseltine, the Deputy Prime Minister, during a lengthy chat in June 1996: "The Deputy Prime Minister is very concerned about this, and so he should be," Guenier said.

He admits his own first reaction was that it could not possibly be true: "It is such a silly problem; it's absurd, but that doesn't mean it isn't a major problem". His investigations in North America convinced Guenier.

Nearly everyone there has a problem, he found. Greater Vancouver regional district council is concerned about the effect of the millennium on everything ranging from maintenance, payment of benefits, payment of staff to calculation of depreciation on the council's capital assets. "We have a lot of older systems that will be affected," said Dinie Kloosterboer, the technology planning supervisor in an interview with the Vancouver Sun in May 1996. "We consider it to be a real problem. We have it booked to work on in the next year and hope it's not too late."

An anonymous technology controller for a state in the US was in despair: "I am relatively new to this problem, but it is so all-pervasive that I've considered leaving rather than dealing with it and getting the bullet when it's not fixed in time." He admitted to keeping a letter of resignation in his computer should his job become too demanding in the next few years. Meanwhile, Rod Armstrong, the State of Nebraska's Information Technology Coordinator, has 12,000 computer programs to deal with, containing 12 million lines of code. Armstrong faces a massive task, and has already discovered that one computer program interprets the numerals '00' in the date field as an error, and shuts down the system. For a state government that is a rather serious glitch. Armstrong's biggest concern is the revenue and accounting systems, and defusing the millennium bomb is proving such a costly project that the state government has decided to divert $11.5 million in state revenue on cigarettes to to pay for part of the task of making the computers millennium-friendly.

"One of the areas of great concern is the ability to collect taxes, issue birth certificates, run businesses, you name it - there are so many implications that it is really hard for us to imagine," Ben Nelson, the Governor of Nebraska, told us at the beginning of September 1996. "Computers are absolutely vital to us - they are as important as the roof over our heads. We are becoming more and more dependent on computers to operate, as I think every organisation is - and some of the computers which we depend on to operate are at risk."

Nelson is one of the few who appreciate the political, economic and technical dangers of inaction on the millennium bug. The Governor has brought together a group of people to work on fixing the problem and offer advice to businesses in the state, which covers a vast rural area. "We have about 1.6 million people and information technology is vitally important to the state as a whole because of its vast geographic size. For the last two years we have been linking people up through information technology and many of our schools are now on the Internet, which will be at risk from the problem and require fixing." In Pennsylvania, Governor Tom Ridge has warned local industry of the dangers of not fixing the millennium bomb, while Dr John Parsa, Alabama's state finance department manager, has described the problem as equivalent to dealing with a monster with nine million tentacles: "and you can't miss cutting off even one tentacle," he said.

At a federal level in America, nearly every major government department has appointed a senior official to deal with the problem and formulate a plan of action. Shirley Chater, the Social Security Commissioner, said her agency first began working on their millennium computer bugs in 1989 and should be ready to use the proper four digit date code ('1996', for example), by 1998. The project will cost $30 million, she told The Washington Post: "One can't just get a software programme that would automate how we do this in one fell swoop. Each has to be changed one at a time, separately." Dean Mesterharm, the deputy commissioner for systems, said the agency want the project to finish by December 31st 1998 so an entire year can be spent checking the computers for glitches.

If Social Security started working on this in 1989, it poses the question why some other government departments in America are yet to start changing code seven years later. And why the Pentagon has left it so late to fix weapons systems and missile control computers. The answer, as many senior officials privately admit, is ineptitude. Senator Daniel Moynihan, a senior member of the Senate Finance Committee, has said he is concerned that the problem "may cause widespread errors in computation of government benefits and taxes". "We recognise the problem could be a potential vote-loser," said a Clinton administration official. "The last thing the President would want is for us to lose votes because of a computer error."

It is evident that both banks and government need to sort out their problems, but even if they can succeed in time they will be nowhere without communications. Today that encompasses far more than just the telephone. It means the whole communications infrastructure that connects computers both nationally and internationally. Communications networks today are operated, managed and repaired by computer software control. It is not so long ago that more than half of the entire United States telephone network went black, put out of action by runaway software triggered by a fault in a single out-of-order payphone. That was long before the millennium bomb detonated. What could happen when that explodes is clear to companies like British Telecom.

BT is a world-leader in its field. Like major telecom firms throughout the industrialised world, it employs tens of thousands of personnel and has turnover in the billions of pounds. It is not just a communications company, but an industry that facilitates business across the nation. Millions of pounds have been invested in the very latest communications and business equipment by BT, and when some of the company's senior officials first heard about the dangers of the millennium bug, it is hardly surprising they wanted to check whether their computers would be affected.

It was as late as November 1995 when Mili Lewis, an executive returning from maternity leave, was given the task of assessing the company's risk by Phil Dance, the customer service system programme manager. Initially, she admits, she was sceptical about the scope of the problem and trawled through computer databases and spoke to experts to 'assess the risk'.

"I was quite taken aback by the size of the problem," she said.

"It wasn't originally viewed as being something that would be too complex. I investigated the extent of the glitch and wrote a paper about it which was shown to the board, and then I begged, stole and borrowed staff to set up a unit to deal with the problem."

Even if the BT board had not initially realised the scope of the problem when they were shown Lewis's memo, they soon accepted it when some of the computers in their supply departments started to fail when entered with five-year contracts expiring after the year 2000. "The computers there just would not accept them as valid dates so the staff had to revert to paper files," said Lewis. "We have fixed them, and we are now fixing personnel and billing systems with five year contracts.

"These problems have really made people sit up and take real notice and we have starting prioritising this and organising a systematic investigation to search through the programs. We intend to protect the business by fixing business critical systems first, but we have to scan every line of computer code within BT, and we have about 100 million lines of code," she said.

BT is able to use some mechanical tools to help - which raises the spectre of computers helping to fix other computers - but much of the work will have to be done by humans, by hand. BT has established a so-called 'core team' who have put together a plan of action to defeat the glitch. It will then be included in the national business strategy of the company, which accepts that money simply has to be found for the team.

Lewis explained: "The core team are thinking strategically, and other people are roped in regularly as and when they are needed. Fixing this has been given a high priority and one of the things that we are trying to do is warn other businesses and the government of the problem because it would be ridiculous if we are millennium-proof by the year 2000 and our customers are not. We have decided that we should be open about this and take a lead on it and we have been working with other organisations such as Sainsburys, British Airways and NatWest to get together and help each other to survive after the end of the decade." BT is also writing to all its suppliers to check what their plans are for dealing with their own Millennium Bombs.

As if Lewis doesn't have enough problems to worry about, she is also concerned about what will happen in October of the year 2000 – even if they do fix the dates in their computers. "There will be other problems when we get to 10/10/2000 because that will be the first time that we reach a 10 digit date. The problem then is that lines of code containing the dates might 'run over' into other lines of code and corrupt them, creating other problems on an equal scale."

According to Lewis, it is only when BT conducts a case-by-case examination that it will be able to fully understand the situation. "Some of our systems are extremely large and difficult to work on and the true costs will not start to work through into our budgets until the end of 1996. "We might have to buy new mainframe computers because they simply might not be able to accomodate the year 2000 so we might have to start again. Some hardware will become obsolete after the year 2000 – there is nothing wrong with it, except it just won't work because of the dates."

The British Post Office is also struggling to cross the millennium. Quite apart from its mail services, thousands of stores handle a wide range of administrative functions from cashing social security benefits to issuing vehicle road tax licences. Because of the magnitude of the task it faces, the organisation has been hunting worldwide for specialist software to help it get round the millennium bomb problem. It acccepts the Year 2000 problem poses serious dangers for its business and its potential survival.

The Post Office 'project' to change its computers is expected to take several hundred man-years to complete, but it only started tendering for consultants to assist with the challenge in June 1996. Mark Fitzhugh, the man in charge of the fix, says there are thousands of machines to be checked but he still hopes to have the job finished by 1998, leaving a year to make final changes and test every program.

Difficulties they might have, but at least BT and the Post Office have started work; many other firms have not even met at board level, let alone started to analyse the problem. In particular, pharmaceutical companies appear to have done very little to detect and cure the glitch in their systems. Any drug company whose computer system uses the two-digit year could well reject and dispose of drugs that are due to expire after the year 2000. Many are already experiencing difficulties with the expiry dates on their packaging and have been forced to shorten the 'use-by' date to 1999, which instantly reduces the life of their stock making it less attractive to chemists and customers.

UTILITY companies are also at risk, and every one of the companies we have discussed so far has one thing in common - they all need electricity. "It is no exaggeration to say that computers run our business," said a spokesman for one of Britain's largest electricity companies. "We have three machines that hum away in a locked room and provide the brain for the entire operation. Turn them off? No way; nobody is even allowed to clean the room because they are so vital."

The Tampa Electric Company of Florida was one of the first to appraise the problem: "The more you get into this, it keeps getting bigger and bigger because the two-digit dating is like a cancer throughout all your applications," said Debi Schaibly, Tampa Electric's Year 2000 project manager when interviewed by Computerworld magazine in December 1995. By comparison, European electricity companies are still blissfully unaware of the risk.

The year 1997 should see an increase in awareness throughout the utility companies, banks and government administrations that underpin modern life. According to the Royal Bank of Scotland, one of the first companies to attack the millennium bomb, the work must then be managed as a major project. Analysis takes six months; a Year 2000 project office has to be set up, and entire new divisions have to be established throughout an organisation to manage the business of defeating the bug.

We have looked at how the millennium bug affects the basic infrastructure of society, without which the home, the workplace and society cannot function. As now becomes evident, there are many more computer problems to solve in the other areas which make up our 'consumer society'.

Chapter Six

YOU CANNOT EAT MICROCHIPS

The effect of the millennium bugs on finance, banking, utilities, communications and government threatens some of the crucial infrastructure underpinning our societies. But how could the millennium bomb directly affect consumer basics like food and fuel? Consider for a moment how stock appears on the supermarket shelves and how the local service station always has gallons of petrol and diesel fuel on tap. There is always a plentiful supply - not since the Middle-East oil crises have we seen queues at gas stations. Supermarket shelves are always filled to overflowing.

The goods supply chain work smoothly because retail managers use computers to keep the supply chain in delicate balance, and herein lies an inherent danger; it can all the more easily be thrown out of kilter if things go wrong with technology. Businesses no longer keep back-up stocks which might cushion them against supply failure.

One of the most important maxims for modern business is the 'just-in-time' theory where companies leave until the last minute the moment when they have to replenish their supplies. A supermarket is actually losing money if it receives extra supplies too early because the new stock takes up valuable storage space and it has to be paid for earlier than necessary, affecting outward cash-flow. Similarly, the petrol station manager wants to sell all his petrol and then have his tanks re-filled at the last possible moment to maximise his revenue - 'just-in-time'. The theory affects every aspect of the long supply chains that ultimately reach all of us. Unfortunately 'just-in-time' businesses will be particularly affected by the millennium bomb.

"Our investigations into 'just-in-time' came about when we realised how many production systems don't really keep stock," said Dave Allen, from the computer giant Logica, which has been working on preparations for the millennium for several years. According to Allen, nobody keeps, for example, six months of washers. If a particular company's washer supply system fails then their washers fail to arrive at the next tier supplier, who cannot put them into, for example, brakes which they then supply to a car plant.

"Suddenly there's no production line working anywhere," said Allen. "I heard of one case study recently which perfectly illustrates the problem. There was a strike at a seat manufacturer supplying a large car company. The cost of the strike to the seat company was huge, but the costs grew massively when the car company was hit because they couldn't get their cars out, and the retailers didn't have any cars to sell. Imagine then what would happen if the millennium bomb was to strike every level; these companies can't simply turn their computers off when they malfunction because of the millennium - in most cases the production lines are computers. What will happen if the people who make the material for the seats fail to supply; what happens if the people who supply the thread for the material fail to supply?

"We don't yet know where the problem would stop but we estimate the millennium bomb could knock out 30-50% of production lines. Production lines in most manufacturing industries are run by computers and could collapse. The danger posed by the millennium bomb cannot be underestimated, it is like nothing we have ever been confronted by." Allen believes the risks extend way beyond the conventional acceptance of the problem: "People must remember that anything with a computer chip could be affected. I would not fly around the year 2000. The risks to computers are that high from the date change. I wouldn't get in an office lift either, but at least a lift is attached to a wire."

Joe Celko, a senior staff consultant with Osoft Development - a consulting company based in Atlanta, Georgia told Infoworld in June 1996 of one example of how 'just-in-time' businesses can be affected. "There was a company that had a just in time ordering system and they put in the system in 1995, with rules for recycling products with an expired shelf life," he said. "The company got in some new products with the expiration date of 2000, which was read as 00. The guys in the warehouse caught it because it showed up as being for the Year 1900.

"But as 1995 went on they added more software to the warehouse, including a just-in-time system that used electronic data interchange to replenish the warehouse. When 1996 hit, the routine software patches they had put in place in 1995 did not work and the system read the expiration date of 2001 as 1901. The system rejected shipments that arrived and reordered new shipments from second-tier suppliers. It went through five cycles of re-ordering before the people in the warehouse caught it. Nothing was thrown out, but the suppliers whose product expiration dates were misread got letters saying their products were being returned and they were being assessed penalties. It took the warehouse people two months to fix it."

Most forecasts do not go so far as to predict that problems will arise in the supply of breakfast food and drink during the first few days of the new millennium. What the experts are warning, however, is that supply chains could quickly collapse as computers shut-down or malfunction. So what about the supermarkets? Do they see the Year 2000 posing any serious problems for their business?

Chris Montagnon is the IT director for Sainsburys, one of Britain's largest chains of supermarkets, and he is far from complacent about the dangers his company is facing: "We are putting a significant amount of our budget into solving this problem," he said. "The initial challenge for me was to make my board aware of the scope of the problem. We had to graphically explain to the board of directors what could happen and we also had to tell them that it is wider than just the Sainsbury IT department and that it will affect every aspect of our business."

Montagnon admits that his board of directors were rather surprised by the news, but when it was all explained they quickly realised the extent of the problem. "We depend very heavily on computers and there is no doubt that this has to be done. We have no choice but to do this work otherwise our systems will not work after December 31st 1999." Montagnon claims he has not yet suffered from sleepless nights worrying about the effects on Sainsburys customers of a computer shutdown, but if the store's computerised supply system failed then it would be extremely difficult to fill shelves with even the bare essentials, let alone the fancier goods that customers demand.

Supermarkets also need to fix their computerised cash registers, many of which operate using just two digits for the year. Check the bill the next time you are in a store. In the largest supermarkets and chains the cash till is an integral part of the entire supply chain, and when we buy a packet of flour or packet of cereal, the cash till actually 'tells' the central ordering computer to send more supplies to make up the stock.

Those stores that have invested millions of pounds in creating highly-complicated ordering systems ('just-in-time') could be badly affected by millennium bugs. Marks & Spencer, one of Sainsburys' main competitors in Britain - would not be quite so badly affected because it is less dependent on computers. But even M&S has been preparing its computers for the millennium since one of its supply computers rejected a consignment of corned beef because its sell-by date was in the next century. The computer interpreted it as being nearly a century old.

"With the approach of the Year 2000 it is possible that computer systems may face problems if they use only two digits to store the year," said a spokesperson for M&S, who disclosed the firm started their investigations into the millennium bug in 1995 and believed most of its systems are free of problems. However, the firm admitted some of its computers will be affected and this will "incur some expenditure"; M&S also consider the bug to be enough of a problem to warrant discussing the issue with their suppliers: "raising awareness so that they too may prevent problems arising".

If these reassurances can be accepted, there is no need for consumers to panic, and no need to stock up on tins of long-life foodstuffs just in case the supermarket shelves run bare. Doubtless the stores would find a way - any way - to get food on the shelves. But supermarkets are being decidedly guarded in their comments on the risks of the millennium bomb, and a number of stores are saying they have no comment to make on their level of 'exposure' to the risk of malfunctions.

Like banks and financial institutions they need to maintain public confidence and to trade on the degree of trust invested in them by their paying customers, who must be assured that they will always have access to the supplies they have come to depend on. Another reason for the stores' guarded optimism would be the possible effect on share prices if news about the scope of millennium bomb and 'fixing' costs were to leak out.

But for many reasons it is important now for the public to know the truth. The structure of our Western societies is based around the permanence of certain industries and services, of which food retailers and supermarkets are just one important part. If organisations fail to deal with the problem, our entire way of life will be affected.

In the words of one director of a top British firm: "When we were confronted by our systems experts on this problem our immediate reaction was to suggest we put it off for a year. Our most senior systems people nodded obediently, but one of the younger guys just blew a fuse in front of us and said we were putting the company's survival at risk. We listened to him, and then we tasked one of the directors to establish the veracity of his claims. Now there can be no doubt, the continuing existence of our economies is dependent on fixing this problem."

THE MOST obvious implications of the Year 2000 for the general public relate to our finances and the security of our money and savings we have invested in pensions and insurance bonds. This industry is particularly secretive about the effects that the end of the decade could have on its computers, but in rare moments of openness officials have admitted they are working furiously to correct basic errors created decades ago. "It is a bit like the movement of a duck or a swan," said one expert. "Above the water they both look totally serene and in control, but under the water they are paddling like mad to keep everything going." Credit card companies - which use two digits to signify the year - are working particularly hard. Credit Saison Co., one of Japan's largest credit card companies, faces typical problems: it used to issue cards with a validity of six years, but now it can only issue them with an maximum expiry date of 31/12/1999.

Banks, brokers and finance houses are being extremely secretive about the millennium bomb, terrified that any bad news could result in a panic withdrawal of funds. This is hardly surprising when they are only just considering the worse case scenarios relating to the world of finance.

At the first level we can imagine 'hole-in-the-wall' automated telling machines, which most of us rely on for 24-hour access to our cash, and time-locks in bank vaults failing to work or open because their computers have corrupted. When the Bank of England was questioned about the time-locks in their own vaults, they responded with the cryptic answer: "If there is a problem now then we are sure there won't be by the end of the decade". Banking insiders tell a story about one major international bank which has discovered that its vault doors need urgent modification if they are to open after 1999. The door was constructed of more than two feet of solid steel, and the bank realised that the only way to get at the computer chips inside was to remove the door and return it to the manufacturers for re-welding. Unfortunately, the bank then realised that – like many other old financial institutions – the bank's headquarters were constructed around the huge vaults, and there was no way of removing the vault-door without destroying most of the building. The experts are still scratching their heads and trying to discover a solution. In that bank, and hundreds of others, computer chips have been programmed to interpret the numerals '00' as an 'interrupt' command that shuts them down. Banks have installed security devices into their machines to prevent hackers stealing money by ordering the computer to spill out all its cash to the next person to use the machine. The millennium bomb could trigger the collapse of these machines.

At the next level of chaos the experts pose equally bizarre possibilities. They foresee computerised accounting systems despatching millions of letters to customers requesting that years of compounded interest be paid on overdrafts. As many banks already demand repayment of funds if their customer is overdrawn for just a few days by sending out letters with red type, we can only begin to imagine the colours they would use for a recalcitrant client who has been overdrawn for nearly a century. Alternatively, anyone with a pension due in some years time might start receiving the first payments early; the pensions computer at both a government and company level might compute their age, decide they are eligible, and start the automatic process of transferring money into their account.

The crucial point is that personal financial computing involves billions of files and transactions a year. The only way to manage the automation of this has been to rely on so much computerised work happening without any human involvement: no buttons have to be pressed, no figures have to be checked, the computer simply does it.

Human involvement is increasingly required only when a process or series of transactions actually needs to be started, stopped, or altered. Finding and rectifying errors can take hours of "beavering away", as one expert puts it, just to change a single mistake in the general files. Unfortunately the millennium bomb would not just affect the individual files; it is as if there was a hidden mistake in an entire filing cabinet of paperwork. It would corrupt the structure that contains the files and which automatically manipulates and controls their contents.

Companies have developed their businesses around the premise that computers will quite happily develop with them, and their core responsibilities and files can simply be changed from computer to computer as systems are upgraded and improved. But when there is a fundamental flaw in the computers, nobody really knows how it will affect each machine until the infection actually makes itself known.

ONE of the biggest nightmares for systems managers is that hidden effects of the Year 2000 infection will not be immediately obvious. They might not be detected until millions of mistakes have been made, by which time files could have been destroyed or clients accounts could have been credited or debited with erroneous amounts of money. A number of firms accept they will have to prepare for the worst and set up a customer service, linked to extra help lines to deal with a flood of customer queries from baffled and angry customers.

We have already described the preparations BT and other telecommunications firms are making for the millennium. If they are not successful, there could be some bizarre effects for the consumer. Just imagine you are far from a loved one on New Years Eve 1999, and you ring them a few minutes before Big Ben strikes 12 in the hope of talking to them - or singing awful songs - as we move over to a new millennium. Unless the phone company computers are cured of their Year 2000 problems, the computers could easily think your call lasted 99 years, and charge accordingly.

As with other large firms, phone company accounting systems could go haywire, sending bills to customers who (the computer would think) have not paid their bills for 99 years. The computers could automatically cut off customers' phones because of more subtle software faults. For the managers of BT, and Mili Lewis in her role as Millennium Programme Manager, the most worrying aspect of the year 2000 problem is its ability to simply stop old computers from working at all. Many of the larger mainframe computers within the company "simply will not work after the Year 2000", according to Lewis. Perhaps now is the time to invest in a CB radio.

Transportation will also be affected by the Year 2000 problem unless a cure is found. Railway computers, which schedule trains according to dates and track their locations, are among the hundreds of thousands around the world that need to be fixed.

Charles Parks, a computer expert who has been put in charge of fixing the machines controlling American Union Pacific Railroad in Omaha, has said he is appalled by the lack of knowledge of the problem and shocked by the lack of technology available to help him and his team of computer-doctors - especially when the problem has been known about for such a length of time.

Lou Marcoccia of New York's Transit Authority has spent the past five years heading up a team working to modify the authority's old computers but he still has thousands of lines of code that must be checked and cured of the bug. "We do not fully understand what would happen if we don't make the changes but we can make certain assumptions based on the fact that computers are vital to our operations and many of them will not work if not modified," said his authority. "We can draw our own conclusions of the effects."

Even the workings of cars can be affected by the date-change, and not just because their manufacturers could suffer from supply problems. Modern cars are packed with computers and computer chips, controlling engine management, anti-lock braking, cruise control, power steering, fault monitoring and service intervals. Some of the most expensive cars have more technology packed into them than early jets.

THE IMPACT of the millennium bug problem on hospitals is particularly worrying, because the world of medicine has embraced technology with the same enthusiasm as the world of finance, with the distinction that lives could be at risk in hospitals if the technology fails. Computers are used for many tasks including the control of x-ray and radiotherapy machines, and in operating theatres for some of the most delicate surgical techniques.

It is to be hoped that vital hospital computers for clinical activity will not be allowed to fail and will, somehow, be cured of their millennium bugs in time. However, there are many other machines dealing with mundane tasks such as ordering drugs and blood supplies. In a commercial company this would be the equivalent of arranging delivery of paper clips and staples, but this type of task becomes life-saving or life-threatening when applied in a medical environment.

The evidence is that most hospitals have been slow to come to terms with the problem, but one that has started work is Meriter Hospital in Madison, Wisconsin. Meriter is a normal 550-bed hospital in the middle of a perfectly normal American city, but it was lucky enough to spot the risks two years ago, and hospital computer experts have been correcting the date error in their machines while working on general maintenance or other projects.

Other hospitals should take note of their lead, because Meriter first spotted a problem when their computers began making errors when asked to compute accounts that went past the year 2000. They realised it would have only been a matter of time before the bugs started to appear in the supply and inventory departments, which could leave doctors short of crucial medications and supplies.

ONE AREA where computer use has expanded dramatically in recent years is in our homes, and not just in the form of shiny new machines that sit on the desks of millions of people who have opted to 'work from home'. Technology has crept through our front-doors in a much more insidious manner: computer chips now control many types of consumer device: from kettles to timed central heating; from air conditioning to answering machines; and from cookers to video recorders. Kitchen appliances have become increasingly sophisticated in recent years with dozens of new functions that have to be controlled by more and more microchips.

It may sound ridiculous, but according to computer experts some of the microchips in these household appliances need to know the correct date to work, and if they do not roll over to the correct time and date on New Years Eve 1999 many could simply seize up. "I know it must seem farcical, but the truth is that nobody really knows what could happen," said one academic. "The thing we must all remember is that anything with a microchip could be at risk – anything: phones, televisions, washing machines."

Readers who have failed to join the computer revolution, and invest in a personal computer, may experience a feeling of perverse satisfaction when they discover that even PCs bought in the last few years could suffer from damaging millennium bugs. The PC has been one of the most common consumer purchases made in recent years yet even some of the most popular models have date glitches. IBM, for example, is only able to guarantee that all its hardware and software will be millennium-friendly from the end of 1996, and other computer companies are further behind. Even now, customers can still go into their local stores and buy a personal computer that will not function properly after the end of the decade.

The effects of computer failure at home may not have such dramatic effects as those in public and corporate systems but will still create real difficulties and inconvenience. Problems will be exacerbated by the fact that many users are recent subscribers to the computer age and are far from computer-literate. They use their computer for personal entertainment and education, or may have just mastered using it to conduct a little business from home. IBM has admitted they simply do not have the resources to cope with the problem and fix every business computer - let alone family machines. They want to 'work with' customers on this and advise them about the changes that need to be made, although what this service might cost is not clear.

It is simply unrealistic to imagine that more than a tiny percentage of owners of personal computers will be able to re-program their own machines to correct millennium date rollover faults of the type we have found to exist, or to easily carry out the installation of new software and hardware 'fixes' to make the machines work past the millennium.

Many people only use their machine for playing games or typing the occasional letter and they have less to fear than other owners. Those who run an office from home, and have to use their computer to keep track of finances, work and business communications, have much more at risk from the millennium bomb. Some of the software installed on machines operates under a license of a fixed period of years, and might have a built-in time code allowing the application to be used for the allotted period and no longer. Unless this is millennium bug-free it may happily function until New Years Eve 1999. But come the new millennium it may suddenly abort, thinking the license is yet to begin because the computer clock has reset to the year 1900.

An application which could be affected is the electronic calendar which people use to drive their on-screen business diary. The millennium bug will not know what day of the week it is, and will tell your diary that Monday is actually Thursday or Saturday is Wednesday. The '00' date may also be recognised as an 'interrupt' where the computer simply stops working altogether. In those cases users will be forced to turn for help to manufacturers and distributors, or any computer expert they can find.

However they will be among thousands of other users complaining and seeking assistance, and there is little chance home users will be considered a priority if company computer systems are failing at the same time.

Chapter Seven

UNSAFE AT ANY SPEED?

Let us leave the millennium bomb to one side for a moment and ask: Do we believe computers are safe? And can we trust them? The answers must be that they are not, and we cannot. The history of computers proves their fallibility, and the situation appears to be getting worse, not better. A number of leading computer experts now openly state that machines should not be trusted with life-critical processes such as the control of trains, planes or nuclear power stations.

But the problem is that in much of the developed world computers have already been entrusted with the complete control of the interlinked operations at the heart of society's day-to-day functioning. We have seen the plans to give computers amazing power with 'artificial intelligence', even linking them directly to human thought. But in the last three decades computers have frequently gone wrong and caused chaos to the mundane operations they control - what could happen if they are given control over functions that really matter?

The situation is more serious than it appears, because there is always an attempt to conceal computer disasters, or, when they do come out into the open, to minimise the consequences. There are those who argue that the computer industry is racing away with itself, running before it can walk. Professor Philip Wadler of the Computer Science Department at Glasgow University believes people should demand higher standards from computer software, which are currently, he says, "appalling". "We need to draw people's attention to the general problems of technology," he continues. "We are just at the beginning of building software and one expert has drawn a parallel with steam engines: when they were first built they would blow up, and this is still happening with computers." Wadler believes that computers will always fail us to some degree, and "we have to decide whether we as a society can cope with these failures. I don't think we will ever be able to build an infallible computer. One reason why the American Star Wars program was cut back was because in order to work it had to work perfectly the first time and that could not be guaranteed. If you build complex systems there is no chance of getting them always right."

The computer programmers might say, "Garbage in, garbage out", and we would be wise to listen to them. They are talking about the commands that control part of the machine, but the comment also applies more generally to project conception and management. Quite apart from the millennium bug, there continue to be many large computer projects which go massively over-budget or assume such a degree of complexity that they can never be completed successfully.

Even under normal circumstances the program that runs first time without a bug, or crashing for some other reason, has yet to be written. The problem with computers is that even after programs have run for years without a bug manifesting itself, the sheer complexity of the program operations can mean that a bug could eventually crash the system when a certain combination of hidden variables arises. Quite what those conditions are, the analysts never know until the malfunction occurs. And in a world of increasing technological complexity, they often only find out what went wrong after the event. Many of these systems are already in place, and many more are being installed.

All of the major world banks, thousands of private companies and all government departments have suffered from the disastrous effects of computer error or failure. In the 1970s the effects of such incidents were limited. In the 1980s their character changed as the use of computers increased and developed, and in the 1990s the potential for disaster has become vastly greater. It is important that we consider the effects of giving computers ever greater potential for widespread disruption.

COMPUTER DISASTERS continue to be associated with the introduction of new computer systems and the resulting need for new software to enter a period of trial and error; and this has not changed in 30 years. Other crashes are caused by the errors of human programmers and operators. Still others are caused by the sheer complexity of programs in which a bug may lie dormant for years. New opportunities for malfunction arise from attempts to repair the damage by extending or patching (putting 'sticky plaster' on) the software, which can introduce further errors. What is so serious about the run-up to 1999 is that all these dangerous situations are now coming together simultaneously. The circumstances that have given rise to computer failure in the last 30 years could now apply all at once.

The same failure stories arise in the 1990s just as they did in the 1970s. Take, for example, wages that do not get paid, although computerisation of wages and salaries in the UK took place nearly three decades ago. The new accounting systems caused problems for no fewer than 85% of companies that implemented them. The London Daily Telegraph reported on one disaster in March 1970, under the headline 'Strike Over Berserk Computer': "More than 600 went home two hours early yesterday in protest at a faulty computer which calculates their wages at the factory of Denis Ferranti meters. Some have been given £97.00 instead of £14.00 whilst other have received only two shillings. 'We are fed up with its unreliability,' said Mr Peter Longden, a shop steward. 'By the time mistakes are found on a Friday it is too late to do anything about it until the following Monday'. Mr Terence Holt, Managing Director, said 'This machine is confounding the management as well when it goes berserk. Sometimes members of staff work till four in the morning to do its work'."

The Telegraph reported again in August 1970: 'Four Thousand Threaten Strike so Computer Gets Sack'. "A computer has been relieved of its wages calculation duties because 4,000 workers have threatened to strike on the grounds that it does not get its sums right. The workers, at the BSA motorcycle factory at Smallheath, Birmingham, claimed that not only was the computer continually going wrong, but that the management failed to offer a satisfactory explanation. Yesterday the management promised to return to a manual system of wage calculation. A BSA spokesman said the pay-roll had been completely computerised for more almost a year. It is now apparent that the testing period was not adequate."

By the 1990s most of the pay-roll programs should have lost their bugs. But the initial problems still occur again and again. In July 1995, 25 years later, the government Treasury computer failed to pay thousands of civil servants. The London Sun newspaper reported: "Judges had their pay stopped yesterday when a government computer went haywire. They are among 2,000 civil servants, including tax men, paid by an accounts centre at Chessington, Surrey. Their wages should have gone to their banks yesterday. It is hoped that they will now be paid on Monday. One unpaid worker said: 'The judges are hopping mad. And I'll have my bank on my back over bills and direct debits.' A Treasury spokesman said: 'This was a minor malfunction'."

But then these mistakes are always classified as 'minor malfunctions'. It is characteristic of those computer crashes that are publicised that spokesmen feel obliged to minimise the incident. Consider the implications of this 'minor malfunction' – thousands of people were not paid their salaries. If a 'minor' malfunction can have this result, what happens with a 'major' malfunction, such as the millennium bomb?

The unpaid government employee is also making a telling point about computerised wages failures in the 1990s: unlike the workers of the seventies at the motorcycle factory, he has to consider the electronic ramifications of not being paid. Here he is not looking at a mistake in the calculation of physical money in the old-fashioned pay packet, he is looking at electronic money that has not been sent to his bank at all. Because his bills and obligations are also controlled by agencies claiming payment electronically through that bank his entire personal economy is at risk.

Computerised banking is now at the heart of financial transactions today. Not only are banks utterly dependant upon computers, but all computerised finance is utterly dependant upon banks. The failure of electronic funds transfer at point of sale, and electronic cash withdrawal, would stop society in its tracks. No one would know who owes what to whom; and it is not as if this type of mistake has not already happened. 'Today' newspaper reported in June 1994 on a Barclays bank fiasco: 'Computer Blunder puts Thousands in Red'. "Thousands of people found they were in the red yesterday after a computer blunder hit every branch of Barclays Bank. Angry customers stormed in demanding to know why wages and other deposits had not been credited to their accounts." It came just three weeks after National Westminster Bank admitted that a 'human error' wrongly debited up to 60,000 accounts.

The Barclays blunder was revealed only when customers

noticed statements were wrong. They were left even more angry and frustrated when clerks told them the computer fault meant it was impossible to tell them their correct balance. "One cashier in Nottingham said: 'To say customers were angry is to put it mildly. They were raging. Some could not even get any money even though they had been paid last week'. As millions of incorrect statements were shredded, Barclays' head office in London promised customers would not lose cash: 'We had a bug in our national computer centre which affected every single branch in Britain. It paralysed every bank's computer from Thursday. All we can do is apologise. It was human error and these things happen. But we would urge our customers to check their new statements very carefully'."

In March 1993 thousands of angry credit card customers jammed telephone switchboards at National Westminster Bank after a computer error redirected money they had paid to clear their bills to other people's Visa accounts. But until newspapers picked up the story, the bank kept quiet about the fiasco and relied upon customers to complain. Only when it had been made public did the bank change its policy and undertake to inform up to 15,000 credit card holders about the computer error at the NatWest credit card centre in Southend, Essex.

As more and more businesses have put their sales through computerised credit processing the complaints from the banks' customers have become both more widespread and more bizarre. Barclays Bank, for example, still does not know why standing orders on every account with the name Fiona were mysteriously deleted on its internal employee accounts. An Australian bank found its customers' cash withdrawal facilities stopped on a Monday morning after it implemented new software over a weekend. Long queues formed at branches of the bank throughout the country.

Computers are portrayed as near perfect devices but after years of swallowing bank claims of computer infallibility, the law courts in Britain have now accepted that phantom withdrawals from automatic teller machines do not necessarily mean the customer has absent-mindedly withdrawn the money, but that perhaps the computer has 'lost' it. The banks are always at pains to minimise the seriousness of software faults. But the fact remains that these errors are taking place as part of normal everyday life with computers.

SOFTWARE is increasingly employed in situations where there is no fail-safe manual back-up system: bank clerk's no longer consult a paper ledger and make an entry with pen and ink. In the same way, machine automation of many aircraft has taken away fall-back safety and put all operations in the hands of computers.

Aircraft today are so densely packed with sensitive electronics that it is not even possible to allow passengers to use mobile phones in case their radiation adversely affects the equipment. With fly-by-wire systems, the pilot moves only an electronic joystick or throws switches, and computer software operates the plane, even some emergency fail-safe systems. It goes still further when the computer autopilot is in charge of many of the flight legs, approaches and landings. So complex is the software process in the advanced European Airbus that two computers are used to make decisions, and a third one to monitor them and override if the first two do not agree.

Bear in mind that the United States space agency NASA has already postponed one space-shuttle flight because it was scheduled to take place over a year end from December to January. The reason? Knowing that computer software is subject to year-end bugs, NASA decided it was safe to fly only in January. If an ordinary year end can be this critical, what about the year end coming in 1999? Would you feel like flying somewhere on that date in a computer-controlled aircraft? Airlines are listening to their advisors and at least three major world airlines are planning to suspend service over the millennium weekend because of fears that aircraft could malfunction.

You may not feel like riding on the world's tallest and fastest roller coaster in Blackpool, north-west England, either. 'The Big One' is computer-controlled by customised safety software so that accidents are 'impossible'. Yet it crashed at the height of the August holiday season in 1994 and injured 26 people because a software error allowed one car on the 70-metre-high ride to smash into the back of the preceding one. The second car should have been held on emergency brakes when the first one stopped ahead of it, but it failed.

Such software is 'safety critical'. It is used to drive not only planes and roller coasters, but nuclear power plants and high-speed trains. Problems arise when the software and the operations it generates are so complex that it is impossible to test exhaustively for every situation which might activate a bug or crash. The only real long-term test is life. Systems are allowed to run on the balance of probabilities: they are reliable, but not infallible, and somewhere deep in that software maze may lie a crash waiting to happen.

In public administration, computerisation and the consequent glitches one has to cope with are further encroaching on our lives. Ever more important decisions are being put in the hands of computer systems. Bill Frost, an ordinary British holiday-maker on his way to the beaches in Spain, found himself banned as an 'undesirable' when he arrived in Malaga from Manchester. On the orders of the computer running the new EU 'Schengen' database system he was put on a flight back to the UK, where he was met by police and immigration officials who held him for questioning. They established that he was neither an illegal immigrant nor an international criminal. Put on another flight back to Spain, he was told he had been the victim of a computer error.

Another group of victims were thousands of young Britons being over-taxed for months after starting work for the first time. Millions of pounds of extra deductions were made from their wages by an Employment Services Agency computer. This particular computer, reportedly the largest non-military system in

Europe, has had plenty more teething problems. Job training scheme changes and benefits introduced by the government as an important plank in its policy recently had to be postponed for six months because the computer software would not have been able to handle them. Parliament and an army of civil servants are helpless at the mercy of bug-ridden software.

The implementation of a computer system to control the journeys of London's fleet of ambulances speeding to accidents and emergencies is a well-chronicled disaster particularly relevant to millennium bomb projects. The London Ambulance Service was told it would get its paramedics to crises around the UK capital faster. Instead, the journeys took hours longer. The programme was one huge crash from beginning to end.

The computer-controlled ambulance despatch system, costing £7.5 million, was a replacement for one which had preceded it and the new model failed. The Guardian newspaper wanted to know why £1.5 million of software proved to be less reliable than human despatchers: "The detailed system design was fundamentally flawed... Systems development was carried out under extreme time pressure with the results that software was delivered late, changes were made without going through proper change-control procedures, and software quality assurance was poor. Up to the day it went live, no attempt had been made to test the operation of the system under anything like realistic loading. A thorough pre-implementation testing strategy is a key aspect of any systems development."

The system lasted one and a half days during which the London Ambulance System failed to get to critical emergency calls. In the end staff insisted on shutting it down. The management made it linger on for a further ten days, such was their hope that the system could be revived. Eventually it was shut down and has never run since – today manual controllers are at their desks with maps and radio telephones, making decisions based on experience and skill. Human operation is possible, and has proved to be a fail-safe fall-back.

The London Ambulance story is significant because it relates to poor management of new software. The programs being developed to cope with millennium bug problems represent a mass of new remedial software development. Like the LAS system this is being done under extreme time pressure, and that pressure will increase as the months pass. It is therefore also likely to encounter the same sort of short-cuts in planning and thorough testing – there may just not be time, even if it gets written at all. The London Ambulance Service could turn their computer system off and go back to human operations; but with many millennium bug applications, there is no human operation possible.

So it is not just computers that are far from infallible, but the software with which they are programmed. The bigger and more complex the program, the greater the pressure of time and the more likely it is that computer software engineering and project management becomes unsound. In July 1996 news leaked out that the British government was investigating how more than £100 million of National Health Service money has been wasted on computer systems that do not work and have either been scrapped or are due to be scrapped. One hundred million pounds represents a huge amount of incompetence: it should convince us that computer systems builders are not the brilliant architects they consider themselves to be, especially when under pressure. And serious pressure is what millennium bomb program replacement is going to be all about.

The computer business will not like being described as an industry out of control. It is led by some of the most brilliant brains in the world. But the millennium bug must give us serious pause for thought about the industry's reserves of common sense. The apparent lack of planning, which has allowed these bugs to survive, may yet turn out to have made computers our worst enemy, because of the runaway pace at which we have allowed this industry to go about its business of transforming us into an information and communications society. For a long time we have been excited and seduced by the mesmerising power of computers, until we no longer drive the software but are driven by the software.

We are in the hands of an industry which has designed and put us at the mercy of a machine culture with a fundamental flaw: because of the millennium bug, it will work only up to a certain date, and then it will stop dead. But this is only a symptom of the larger problems. Clever computer people have dazzled themselves with their own computer brilliance, and they have engaged us with a never-ending series of high-speed developments: new, better and faster hard disks, pentium chips, CD-Roms, games, bells, whistles, productivity, E-Mail and the Internet. They have hypnotised us with speed, electronic management, storage, marketing, databases, electronic money and administrative and business power. And in so doing, they have conveniently forgotten that none of it will work properly on the stroke of midnight when the glittering carriage turns into the proverbial pumpkin.

Chapter Eight

SHOULD WE LOVE COMPUTERS?

Do you love your computer? Could you place your hand on your heart and claim you enjoy its presence and power, and promise it solemn allegiance as long as you both shall word process? Or do you dare to be one of the many who actually harbour deep suspicions about the infernal machines, and the way they have reached into our lives and taken control? If you have ever considered tipping a pot of coffee over the keyboard that dominates your desk at work, fear not, for you are still in the majority. In the course of talking to hundreds of people about the millennium bug we found plenty of support for a surprisingly backward idea – a society with fewer computers.

Some might find pressing keys a substitute for human interaction, but most of the public still want computers to be kept in check. And the millennium bomb could be just what they are looking for to put the brakes on the computer industry. Robin Guenier, head of the British government's taskforce on the Year 2000 problem, believes there is now a "real risk" of a massive backlash against computers by a public disgusted at the damage such a simple problem could cause. "It should have been fixed years ago," he says with a shake of his head.

"Computer gurus have spent the last decade assiduously cultivating their power bases within their organisations," he told the magazine Computer Weekly in August 1996. "They have worked long and hard to transform the image of information technology from one of expensive, boring, back-room boffinry, into the command centre of the corporate ship. Now all that is at risk thanks to the year 2000 date change problem."

The magazine pointed out that, after clawing their way to the door of the boardroom, some computer managers will now have to face an angry board of directors asking this question: "Why are you presenting us with a global bill of anything up to half a trillion dollars to fix a problem that will confer no competitive advantage at all, which you have known about for over 20 years, and which you yourselves created in the first place?". Not even the most gifted computer manager can make up for the years of apathy and procrastination during which time the millennium problem has grown bigger and nastier. The "wounded are bleeding", said the voice of British computing.

PERHAPS we should examine one of the most important developments in society in the last few years: the Internet. Even in an industry dominated by exaggeration and unfulfilled expectation, no concept has ever generated so much hype, or so much annoyance among users. For the uninitiated, the Internet is the world's biggest computer network with millions of machines linked by satellite and landline to create the Information Superhighway, offering users access to a communications revolution that enables many to throw off the shackles of corporate employment and work from home in direct contact with clients or employers. But the Internet is a bubble close to bursting, with many companies involved in the business going bankrupt or suffering severe financial problems, and the Internet has come under fire for not living up to the initial claims of its supporters. True, there are wonderful 'toys for boys', from new on-line magazines and shopping to on-line advice sessions and banking; but part of the problem with the 'Net and, perhaps, with computers more generally is that it is the boys who are doing most of the embracing, with research indicating that nearly 95% of Internet users are male, with 80% of the users under the age of 35.

Society as a whole has not embraced this so-called communications revolution: women are largely being excluded, partly because of their lack of interest in computers and partly because they can see that new technology is not as exciting as many claim, according to university academics who have studied computer use.

But does it really matter if the Internet is dominated by one particular group of men and others are excluded from the Information Superhighway? Those who support the idea of a 'wired world' admit that their greatest fear is that the Superhighway will become the global information provider, with a monopoly on the dissemination of crucial national and societal issues. If you are not connected to the Net, so the thinking goes, you will have no political influence – you will be outside the goldfish bowl. But is this really true? A new generation of children may well be passing through schools where an education in the use of computers is considered fundamental to the development of a rounded individual, but are we really to believe that the politicians and civil servants who lead us will soon remove themselves from the normal processes of government to the relative isolation of a computer village? It seems unlikely given the present low level of Internet users, despite some excitable predictions of a billion users world-wide within the next few years. So long as only a minority want to subscribe to the Information Superhighway, then only a minority of information will be channelled down its wires.

Businesses rushed to exploit the commercial possibilities opened up by the Net, but at the moment the Net is used for little more than titillation, and the most frequently visited 'sites' are those offering pornographic pictures or using sexually explicit language. More worryingly, the Net is being exploited by political extremists, racists and criminals who recognise its potential for anonymous recruitment and control of illegal activities.

A sub-culture is emerging, fostered by the Internet, where, for example, far-right American organisations can spread their propaganda quickly and quietly around the world to a network of supporters whose only links are through their computers. The Institute of Jewish Policy Research (IJPR) has monitored the explosion in racist material on the Internet and World Wide Web – the most interesting area of the Internet, where groups can put up 'posters' for other computer users to read and even listen to recorded information. David Capitanchik, a leading academic from Aberdeen University in north-east Scotland, studied the Internet for the IJPR and has expressed concern that inflammatory material will become instantly available to children and students when the Net, and through it the World Wide Web, become widely available in schools and colleges.

But it is not just political extremism that the Net is successfully fostering. Smut and pornography proliferate on the Web as they do in no other medium. Within seconds of logging-on to the Internet, anyone can view obscene images by simply inputting a few words and telling their computer to search for any mention of a particular subject. Photographs are swapped by computer users, with special enthusiasm being reserved for snaps of naked celebrities or hard-core pornography. "I might sound like a pervert, but does anyone have pictures of naked Hollywood stars when they were kids?" asks one anonymous Web-user in a bizarre plea to other like-minded users.

The anarchic structure of the Web means there is very little interference or control, a boon to supporters of free-speech, but a cause for serious concern among the police and those who consider that society must be protected from its more extreme elements, whatever their constitutional or legal rights.

Dr Donna Hughes, a lecturer in women's studies at Bradford University, has exposed one of the most appalling uses of the Internet: the international trade in women. If you want a Polynesian bride or a prostitute in Brussels, the Internet is the new place to look. Users can call up on-line catalogues of hookers and prospective wives which provide full photographs, descriptions, and the various prices that pimps or relatives will accept to sell off the vulnerable young girls.

All tastes can be catered for, even paedophilia and necrophilia, says one Belgian policeman who has investigated the extent of criminal activity on the Net. "Much of it may not be illegal, but it certainly raises very serious moral and ethical concerns. We have to consider what we are allowing, rather than just sitting back on our hands and only considering the rights of those who are using the Net. The rights of those affected by the spread of such information must also be an important consideration."

So perhaps those who are still ignoring the Net, the Web, the Superhighway and all the other supposed benefits of computerization are not quite so foolish as many in the industry would have us believe. Few outside the computer industry will care if the whole structure is brought crashing down by the millennium bomb.

THOSE still in the (ever-shrinking) majority who do not own a home computer probably encounter the machines in their workplace, where the history of the computer is chequered by fear and suspicion. Research by stress management experts has discovered that office computers are a major cause of absenteeism and anxiety; they also make many office workers feel completely irrelevant. It is not difficult to see how computer-envy can strike down

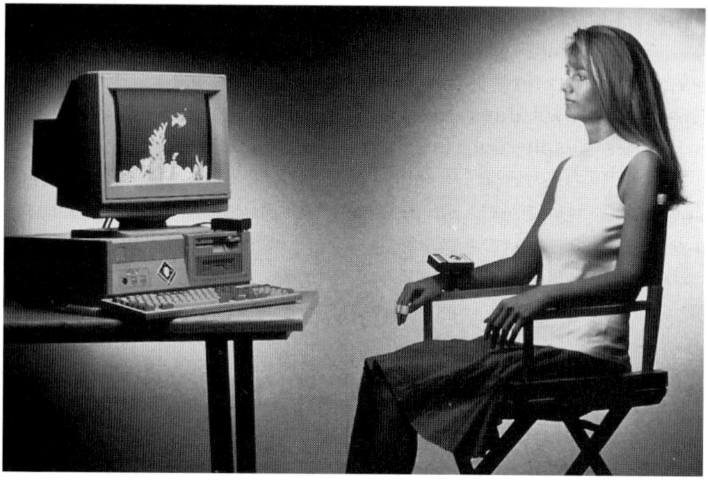

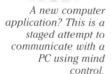

A new computer application? This is a staged attempt to communicate with a PC using mind control.

those unprepared for the rapid computerisation of offices and jobs. Immune from the constant battle to maintain morale in the face of redundancies, poor canteen food and wicked managers, the company computer hums along quietly in its air-conditioned, spotless room, guarded by computer technicians who speak the impenetrable language of technology. The worker bees may be expendable, but if the computer wanted to be hand-fed exotic fruits, management would be forced to comply.

"There is a divide between those who can use computers and those who cannot, and obviously the younger generation accept computers more than older workers," said Elspeth Brown, who works for a large advertising agency. She is typically sceptical about their uses. "I suppose it's because younger people view them more as part of the office furniture. They are no more annoyed by a systems crash than a broken chair because they are more used to computers going wrong and don't remember what the work-place was like before computers took hold." According to Brown her office computers regularly fail, and it takes an engineer from outside to get the machines working again. "They don't tell us what they are doing to fix them, and I don't want to know."

Advertising is a business in the throes of constant change and development and agencies, just like organisations in any other sector of business, want to be seen as at the cutting edge. However Brown does not feel particularly intimidated by the machines, despite only learning to use them properly when she was working on her university dissertation: "I'm not great on computers but I learn what I need to know just to get on with the job. There is no point in learning anything more, because the technology of today is quickly superseded by the technology of tomorrow."

Tim Denton, from a large international sales and marketing-company, also believes they are little more than status symbols: "Companies are very conscious of wanting to be innovative and sometimes they introduce computers without fully knowing what they can do. A lot of money is invested and it puts a huge onus on the staff because managers want to justify the expenditure by quickly proving the viability and importance of the technology." Denton can illustrate the point by describing the problems he has had with a new computer introduced into the office. "It doesn't do its job properly and is constantly going wrong, making the people who work in the same department look incompetent, when it is actually the fault of those who failed to test it and modify it for its particular task."

Denton is relatively ambivalent about the machines but the same cannot be said for Jonathan Hartnell, who works for a publishing company and commutes between the firm's offices in Britain and France. "I do not like computers, I do not trust computers and I have absolutely no desire to understand how to work them apart from knowing the basics," he said. Hartnell is young, energetic and resourceful, a man whose job it is to spot and develop potential in others. Why then does he not see computers as a helpful colleague or friend? "Put it this way, my assistant and I spent two hours this afternoon trying to work out how to print out multiple labels on the damned machine. It would have been quicker if we'd found an old quill and ink and crafted them ourselves. You learn one set of instructions for one computer and then you need to learn another set of rules for the next one. It's such a waste of time and I just don't need the hassle."

Hartnell and countless others believe that many of their problems with computers are due to over-sophistication of many software programmes. He simply wants to be able to tap his keyboard and watch the letters and figures appear on the screen, then press another button and watch it print out. He will only use a tiny amount of the potential of his machine but then statistics, even those released by the computer industry, show that the majority of computer users use no more than ten per cent of their potential.

Why does the computer industry make such complicated products? The answer is partly that they have the technology and, as we saw in earlier chapters, the impetus is always for improvement. Of equal importance is that a substantial part of the software business lies in selling upgrades. However, as the packages grow in complexity and in memory requirement, they become ever more susceptible to bugs. The computer industry believes big is beautiful but, as Robin Guenier said, it could find the Year 2000 problem creates a crisis in public confidence.

Individuals with a profound dislike of computer technology are growing in number. They are the New Luddites or neo-Luddites, and they are a loosely organised movement opposed to computers and technology. Their inspiration was Ned Ludd, who rose up in opposition to the industrialisation of Britain in the 19th century. His followers saw how new machinery had been introduced by their callous employers and taken their jobs as weavers. The Luddites often unceremoniously smashed the machines to pieces after conducting mock trials presided over by weavers who would condemn technology 'to death'. There were riots and public disorder ending with the execution and transportation of protesters. 'Luddite' has since become a term of casual abuse, a verbal poke in the eye for someone not thought to be capable of moving with the times and adapting to changed circumstances.

Besotted with computers? This businessman has been equipped with an 'Arm Office' – a tiny portable PC and communications system.

The theory that technology destroys not only jobs but also the quality of life is gaining a popular hold in Europe and America. Many neo-Luddites have embraced the Internet for mass communication to propagate their manifestos, conferences and a strong belief that in elevating technology to the role of decision-maker, society has taken a potentially harmful path.

Christian Taylor, a young ecologist at Bath University in south-west England, has tried to raise neo-Luddite awareness among fellow scientists at international conferences. "I think we can draw an analogy between our societies and a man sweeping a street with a brush and a man with one of these spanking new street-cleaning robots that they push around our cities," he said. "In one case we have a tool requiring a lot of muscular effort to perform a task. Compare that with the man who has the robot, where it is effectively the man who is the tool helping the machine to do a task that society has determined is better for machines to perform than for man. Technology is evolving as our master." Taylor, an erudite and active campaigner for the environment, has visited India to warn villagers not to 'Westernise' their lives and lose their unique cultures. Only half-jokingly he suggests, as do some other like-minded scientists, that machines will one-day 'rediscover' little humans inside them, as we now discover bacteria inside us. "What we have to decide," says Taylor, "is whether we see the future as some sort of computer-controlled cyborg world, or a more equitable one."

Kirkpatrick Sale, a New York-based author, academic and lecturer, destroys computers with a sledge-hammer in front of his students to show they are vulnerable, fragile, and far from sacred devices. Sale, who recently published a history of the Luddite movement, 'Rebels against the Future', believes the ranks of neo-Luddites will swell even more in the next few years as the risks and dangers of the computer age become increasingly obvious – and the millennium bomb reinforces everything they believe.

Such anti-computer sentiments are supported by research released by one of the world's leading experts on the use of computers, Professor Thomas Landauer of the University of Colorado, who has challenged conventional wisdom to argue that computers are of far less benefit to society than we all imagine. It is a radical reappraisal of beliefs installed in us by education and every media, but Landauer has researched his theories thoroughly. He contends we have spent £1,000 billion on computers world-wide during the past 35 years – most of it since the middle of the 1970s. And yet, during the same period, the productivity of the world's major economies has fallen to less than half that of the years immediately after the end of the Second World War.

According to Landauer, computers do not yet perform enough useful tasks and are too complicated and difficult to use. The technology is also comprehensively misused and applied to the wrong tasks. In an eloquent study of the impact of computers, 'The Trouble with Computers' – published in 1995 by the Massachusetts Institute of Technology Press, Landauer claims there appears to be no real link between the amount of money a company spends on computer technology and its subsequent financial success. This applies to large conglomerates and small family businesses. According to the Professor, society has paid vast sums for computerisation but is not receiving the expected returns.

Even word processors for letter-writing gain his criticism because only a small amount of an employee's time is actually spent typing. Even if a computer word processor improves the speed and efficiency of a typist by, say, 80 per cent (as many studies suggest), the benefit to the entire firm in overall productivity would be in the region of just three per cent.

He applies the same critique to automated cash machines outside banks. Though they have improved waiting time for the general public, he argues they have achieved little in productivity terms because transactions comprise such a small part of a bank's overall activities. Landauer also makes an important point about the ever-increasing list of functions that computer programs can perform after he watched senior computer scientists struggling to master their intricacies. Learning the most basic 'manoeuvres' took those experienced computer experts several days of trial and error. If they had problems, how can the rest of us hope to take command of these infernal machines?

Chapter Nine

THE DANGER OF SABOTAGE

Before the full dangers of the coming new century became apparent, the greatest threat to computers was thought to come from hackers and 'virus-writers'. These terms describe two enemies of computer society: those who break into other people's computer systems electronically, and those who write software programs which sabotage the operations of the computers they infect.

Virus-writers are perhaps the more dangerous of the two. Their passion is to write highly destructive computer programs which are unwittingly passed from computer to computer before they are triggered by a specific action, date or event; the program then becomes an active virus, perhaps destroying some vital files, perhaps simply flashing up a sign on the screen to indicate that the machine is playing host to a malevolent rogue element.

The writers of viruses – which have names such as Pathogen, Queeg, Michelangelo and, even, the Barry Manilow Virus (which plays the singer's hits through built-in computer speakers) – are often adolescents, and they have a tendency to give themselves glamourous names such as 'the Black Baron', 'Nukes', 'Brain Damage' or 'The Dark Avenger'. At first their viruses were distributed on floppy disks hidden among seemingly innocent programs; more recently they have been spread on the Internet via electronic mail and bulletin boards.

Hackers prefer to see what damage they can personally inflict on companies and governments by gaining illegal access to sensitive computer files or secret information. Many of them are boys under the age of 20 also suffering from a lack of contact with their peers, and they give themselves names such as the Data-stream Cowboy. While both hackers and virus-writers might sound like juveniles in need of more friends and a couple of parties, their electronic vandalism can have quite astonishing repercussions.

It is something of a perverse credit to the efforts of the virus-writers that some leading scientists and philosophers believe that their creations should be treated as a new form of life. Professor Stephen Hawking, the Cambridge University astrophysicist and mathematician, told a computer conference in Boston in 1994 that the computer viruses share enough of the attributes of natural viruses to be classified as a proper form of life. They might have no metabolism but they exist parasitically and fulfil most definitions of a lifeform, although they are an indictment of humanity's effect on the planet. "It says something about human nature that the only form of life we have created so far is purely destructive," said Hawking. "We've created life in our own image."

Although they have certainly caused untold damage, computer viruses have never quite lived up to the dire predictions of security experts who warned that society would be 'brought to its knees' by computer infections. The initial rash of viruses sparked such a commercial industry in anti-virus software that, almost as fast as viruses have been introduced, detect-and-clean programs evolved to cope with them. However in recent years several viruses have been discovered which have convinced many experts that a virus could be invented from which there is no protection. Just as in the real world, where we are in some cases just one antibiotic away from untreatable viral infections, in cyberspace computer viruses could become more powerful than any technology that exists to defeat them. Until then, the 'cyber-cops', such as the Computer Crimes Unit at New Scotland Yard, and the reporting systems for updating anti-virus software (like 'Doctor Solomon'), have to keep one step ahead of their quarry, like doctors or chemists working against medical bugs.

The host or carrier of a computer virus can be a humble floppy disk or a section of the Internet. An office worker might add a program – a game, an executive toy, a disk from a PC outside the company – only to discover later that the disk has a bug lurking within it. The computer virus can infect an entire machine but lie dormant within it waiting to jump to another computer. When the worker inserts another disk, the bug jumps into it and passes to another machine, then another and another. A PC user might want to store a particular image onto his computer that he has spotted on the Internet, perhaps a picture or a scientific text from a distant university. He downloads the image or the text – but the bug goes with it, and enters his machine. Sections of the Internet which appear perfectly harmless can have viral infections lurking within them, out of sight of even the most experienced computer-doctor.

Just as, over the years, anti-virus software has improved, so the viruses themselves have become more sophisticated and more destructive. The activity of viruses ranges from the purely mischievous to the destruction or modification of files. 'Michelangelo' is one of the most famous viruses, striking every year on March 6th (the artist's birthday). Older infections are Cascade, which causes letters to fall to the bottom of the screen, and Maltese Amoeba, which destroys the software of a host computer while

Computer chips inside a modern PC. Millennium date problems can lurk inside them waiting to cause chaos at the start of the new century.

the poem 'Auguries of Innocence' by William Blake appears on the computer screen. Not all are so pretentious. 'Jerusalem' is an Israeli virus that starts to destroy any infected computer program on Friday the 13th; 'Frodo' is named after a character created by the author J.R.R.Tolkein, and starts to destroy an infected computer on September 22nd. More recent a 'macro' virus has appeared which hides within Microsoft Word files, and causes destructive modifications from within a document.

Perhaps the most alarming aspect of computer viruses is that, despite their youth, the perpetrators can use their abilities to wreak havoc in machines which are supposed to run crucial parts of our economies and social infrastructure. Even Britain's most advanced nuclear power station has not been immune. Personal computers at Sizewell B in Suffolk, a pressurised water reactor, were infected with something known as the 'Yankee Doodle Dandy' virus, which plays the annoying tune and causes computers to malfunction and crash. The virus is thought to have been released on the world by a Bulgarian computer programmer and although it is unclear how Sizewell B's computers were infected, an engineer was sacked following the problems; it is highly likely that the bug was on a computer file which the engineer installed in his office computer – against strict instructions. But fear not, said

Nuclear Electric, which was building the reactor, there was no danger to the public because it was impossible for 'administrative' computers to pass a virus onto the computers which protect the core of the reactor from overheating or meltdown.

The House of Commons has been hit by a virus. Researchers in the Parliamentary library, which serves MPs and provides them with much of their information, became concerned about one of their computer systems when files started to go missing temporarily, were corrupted, or simply disappeared altogether. A computer doctor was called in, but initially he could find nothing wrong. It was only when he took some of the files away and subjected them to a thorough analysis that he discovered one of the most destructive viruses ever seen.

Mysteriously, the only real clue to its existence was the single word 'Nomenklatura', a Russian term describing people qualified for high office in the Communist Party. Although it was never fully proved, detectives believe the virus was devised by another Bulgarian computer programmer, operating out of the country's capital, Sofia, who uses the name 'The Dark Avenger'. What the virus-writer is avenging is unclear because his identity it not known. Despite writing more than 20 highly destructive viruses the Dark Avenger has never been caught, despite the attempts of police forces in the West. He operates with virtual impunity because virus-writing has never really been considered a crime in Bulgaria.

Other virus victims in Britain have been IBM, every major bank, the Home Office and the Foreign Office. In America and continental Europe the picture is the same: viruses wreck havoc. Hospitals and universities are particularly vulnerable to attack because of the number of different people who can access the system and customise it for their own personal use. One British hospital lost vital medical research in a viral attack, while an Italian hospital lost nearly a year's vital AIDS research.

Elsewhere around the world, army computers were devastated by a virus attack in Uruguay, and a survey by a Tokyo accountancy firm discovered that dozens of Japanese firms have gone out of business in the last five years after their computer records were destroyed by different viral infections. The first few viruses, invented in the 1980s, may have been relatively harmless, with simple titles such as 'Stoned', which would cause a sign to pop up on a computer screen saying "Your computer is now stoned!", but the rogue computer programmers have now become more spiteful, and hundreds of new viruses are discovered each year. The police response has been limited by the nature of the crime: tracing the culprits is exceptionally difficult.

In 1993 however, Scotland Yard did achieve one considerable success against a group of virus-writers who called themselves the Association of Really Cruel Viruses. The homes of four of the group – aged from 15 to 25-years-old – were raided in a joint police operation around the country. Although the group's viruses were initially relatively harmless, some of their more destructive creations spread across the world via electronic bulletin boards which were originally designed to enlighten and educate computer users.

Companies are also vulnerable to attack by disgruntled former employees, and many have been embarrassed at the damage caused by so-called 'logic bombs' left behind in company computers by systems experts who knew they were about to be made redundant. One computer whiz-kid installed a logic bomb inside the computer of a firm where he was working after both sides fell out in a dispute over money. The company computers then refused to give employees access to files and the business of the firm was severely hampered. In another case in Paris, a temporary employee who had been brought in by a top firm of lawyers to maintain the company's computers on a salary of £1,000 per week secretly created programs to wipe out colleagues' computer files at night. The programmer wanted to pay off gambling debts and realised that the company would need him to fix the malfunctioning computers.

The damaging bugs cost the firm an estimated £500,000 and

caused morale within the offices to plummet – hardly surprising when lawyers and researchers were arriving at their desks every morning only to find that cases they had been working on for the past few weeks had disappeared into computer ether.

AS MORE powerful computers become cheaper and the knowledge of how to wreak havoc is more widely disseminated, so viruses become ever more threatening. One virus-writer caught recently was responsible for the two highly sophisticated viruses, according to the detective who managed to track him down. The 'Pathogen' and 'Queeg' viruses he created baffle almost every kind of software used to detect them because they change their characteristics every time they infect a new program; just like a mutated human virus, they are actually able to change and develop to avoid capture. The Pathogen virus would strike a computer only on Mondays between 5pm and 6pm, and only if the computer user has opened infected programs at least 32 separate times. Initially the virus appears just as a picture of a keyboard on the screen, then it displays the message: "Smoke me a kipper, I'll be back for breakfast... unfortunately some of your data won't."

The other virus, Queeg, attacks in a similar way, but on Sundays between 12 noon and 1pm, and it displays the message: "Queeg copyright the Black Baron 1994 – featuring Smeg version 2.0. Better than life...". All very bizarre. Smeg stands for Simulated Metamorphic Encryption Generator, and this lets both viruses 'change' themselves, making them extremely difficult to detect. The virus-writer who invented Pathogen and Queeg also developed Smeg, and was lauded by other virus-writers, to whom he passed copies of the viruses so they could also cause huge amounts of damage.

Computer experts had only just finished analysing Queeg and Pathogen when it was announced in late 1995 that an even more serious virus had appeared. 'Concept Nuclear', one strain of the new infection, quickly appeared in Britain, where it managed to outwit most normal software virus-spotters. One London-based charity unwittingly picked up a copy of the virus when one of their workers was downloading information on the Internet about French nuclear tests in the Pacific. The charity had seen warnings in the press about the virus and ran a standard virus check on their computer which spotted that something was wrong, even though the computer could not be sure exactly what. The charity thought the disk containing the virus was probably harmless but still decided to show it to Reflex Magnetics, a group of experts on computer viruses, 'just in case'.

One of Reflex Magnetics' trouble-shooters loaded the disk onto a powerful computer to check it, only for the virus to quickly infect the machine, destroy the workings of the machine's hard drive, and turn an expensive piece of computer hardware into a useless piece of machinery. Concept Nuclear was written in a different type of computer language from most other viruses, making it potentially disastrous for many companies.

Microsoft, the computer giant whose products would be particularly at risk from viral infections such as Concept Nuclear, took a deep breath and announced it would start work immediately on developing a computer test to seek out and destroy the new infection. Microsoft products appear to have been picked-on by a number of virus-writers because the firm was the target of yet another bug, this time called 'Prank', which attaches itself to files written in Word, Microsoft's word-processing system. Prank was seen as a serious threat because word-processing files are regularly swapped between machines, and it would continue to replicate almost continuously.

Perhaps the most bizarre computer virus, and one which was never really designed to be destructive or cause anything but headaches to users, is the 'Fu Man Chu' virus, which has two functions. When the computer is started up the virus clears the screen and then slowly writes across it: "The world shall hear from me again!", which some readers may remember from the Fu Man Chu films. Then the virus searches through text stored in the computer, looks for the names of certain politicians, and adds an insult in a space beneath.

FROM HIS base in Buenos Aires an Argentinian secret agent used a powerful computer to hack his way into top secret computer files belonging to the US Navy, the Pentagon and NASA. "I've infiltrated the US Navy, I've seen inside submarines and much more," said the spy in secret tape recordings. "I could very easily have wiped out files and rubbed out information."

But the hacker was no real spy, and this wasn't a major attempt at international espionage. It was just Julio Cesar Ardita, a 21-year-old computer hacker sitting at a PC in his bedroom at his parents' flat in a middle-class district of Buenos Aires and using his little machine to work his way into some of the most secret computers in America. Exactly how he managed it is still the subject of investigation, but American federal agents obtained a court order allowing them to bug the Internet to track down and trap the young student. Argentinian investigators then monitored Ardita, and caught him apparently admitting all in telephone calls to his girlfriend. In April 1996 the US announced that it wanted to extradite Ardita to America for interrogation.

Ardita is just one of tens of thousands of hackers operating around the world in a voracious hunt for knowledge – the more secret the better. According to the US government there were more than 250,000 attempted intrusions into the Pentagon's computer systems via the Internet in 1995, a quite extraordinary figure that was one of the reasons the Clinton administration set up a special taskforce to assess the risk to the infrastructure of America (including phone, electricity and water supplies) from so-called 'cyber terrorists'.

Ardita managed to obtain information about secret nuclear installations and the entire American defence program after starting his quest in the spring of 1995. Allegedly, Ardita began by using the Internet to access computers at Harvard University, and from there he 'jumped' to computers at the top secret Los Alamos National Laboratory, the US Navy's Research Laboratory in Washington, and its Control and Ocean Surveillance Centre in San Diego. As if that wasn't enough, he also managed to enter computers at NASA's Jet Propulsion Laboratory, until security officials within the US Navy discovered that a few odd files had been planted in some of their most sensitive computers, with names such as 'Pinga' and 'Zap'.

These files contained what are known as 'sniffer' programmes, which can copy vital information and send it down a modem line to another computer. Sniffer programmes are often used by hackers to monitor for changes of passwords, so that if a user of the computer decided to change their password the sniffer program would quietly watch what was going on, note the new password, and then pass it on to the hacker so that he or she could still have access to the computer.

Federal investigators were called in, and they traced the sniffer program back to Harvard University, where they discovered other sniffers in research computers. The investigators then arranged the first-ever court order allowing them to track down the hacker through the Internet using the cyber-space equivalent of a telephone tap.

An incredible 10 million bits of information flood into Harvard University every second, and the team of investigators used a super-computer to search through every single one looking for 15 key words that they thought might enable them to trap their prey. The laws on electronic eavesdropping meant they could only look at a small part of the text of any message containing the key words, but they eventually managed to pick up the methods their hacker was using, and then 'followed' him through the computer wires to Buenos Aires.

The hacker's father is a retired military officer, and he was far from impressed by security at the American installations his son had managed to access: "Obviously the North Americans are not very clear about the security of their systems if a kid from South

American can enter it. I would be ashamed to admit it," snorted Julio Rafael Ardita indignantly to 'The Washington Post'. He has a point, but perhaps Ardita's parents should have been slightly more suspicious of whatever their son was up to in his bedroom for hours at a time – he was running up an international phone bill of $1,500 a month.

Cases such as Ardita's are far from rare. Approximately 160,000 of the 250,000 attempts to enter Pentagon computers mentioned above were deemed to be 'successful', but the US government has refused to explain the possible level of damage the hackers have caused. According to a report by the US General Accounting Office (GAO), commissioned by the Senate Governmental Affairs Subcommittee, the incursions are either just an expensive nuisance – or a threat to national security on a potentially catastrophic scale, depending on your view of the importance of computers. An element of panic can be seen developing among senior US government figures as they realise the damage that can be caused by hackers, the millennium bomb and a dozen other computer glitches, break-downs and failures.

Janet Reno, the US Attorney General, has proposed establishing a sort of computer 'emergency response unit', called the Cyber Security Assurance Group, which would "investigate assaults on our national security" via the Internet. The problem facing such a team is vast: experts testifying before US national hearings on computer security in June 1996 said they believe the world-wide cost from hackers could be colossal. The cause of all these problems? The Internet – the last couple of years have witnessed a tenfold growth in the number of companies and individuals using the Net, which gives hackers, especially those working from less developed countries, the perfect cover to keep themselves hidden from the scrutiny of the authorities.

The US Government's greatest worries do not, however, stem from individual young men using home computers in Buenos Aires. What really keeps officials awake at night is the risk of terrorists or 'hostile states' attacking the communication systems which are crucial to world trade via the Internet, and possibly crippling entire economies. The irony is stark: the Internet was originally set up by the military as a communications system of last resort, one that could still allow messages to flow between nuclear installations and military bases after a nuclear war with the Soviet Union, when other forms of communication had failed. Communications and messages sent via the Internet find a way – any way – to get to their destination, taking whatever route is available for them to make their connection. But the end of the Cold War has opened up the system to the public, who have joined with dizzying speed.

Those officials now suffering from computer-induced insomnia are probably repeating the words of the GAO report in their sleep: "Because the US economy, society and the military rely increasingly on a high-performance networked information infrastructure, this presents a set of attractive strategic targets for opponents. In some extreme scenarios, studies show that terrorists or other adversaries could seize control of defence information systems and seriously degrade the nation's ability to deploy and sustain military forces."

The CIA considers the threat from cyber-terrorists to be only slightly less worrying than the threat of attack by nuclear or chemical weapons. John Deutch, the CIA's director, has said that America is "likely" to face some "very large and uncomfortable" disruption of its most vital computer systems within the next few years. It gets worse: between January and June of 1995 the US military staged military exercises with their computers to help imagine what would happen if an enemy power used the information system to attack the US or its allies. They created hypothetical situations where trains were placed on the same tracks by enemy agents who hacked into transport computers, telephone systems were destroyed by agents dropping logic bombs into machines via the Internet, and weapons systems were paralysed by computer viruses. The tests did not augur well for the US, and revealed what the government admitted were "a number of areas where we have left dangerous gaps in our defences".

There seems to be a real espionage problem. The FBI has also been monitoring the attempts of foreign spies to recruit computer whiz-kids who they can use to hack into US defence computers. They already have several cases to study, one of which involved the 'Data-stream Cowboy', a 16-year-old lad from London who hacked into US defence systems and actually managed, in the words of security officials, to "take control" of the entire computer network at Rome Laboratory in New York State, the top US Air Force research centre, which works on weapons systems, radar and artificial intelligence. The Pentagon admitted that all the laboratory's 33 sub-networks were knocked out and the cost of the incursion was at least half a million dollars.

The Data-stream Cowboy managed to steal top-secret files explaining how commanders of the US Air Force would relay intelligence and targeting information during a war. The USAF eventually managed to trace the hacker to London; a squad of detectives raided his parents' home and the boy curled up on his bedroom floor and cried when he realised he had been caught. He has never been properly charged for his hacking, and investigators believe he may have been prompted into his actions by a mysterious foreign agent known only as 'Kuji', whom the boy talked to via the Internet but never actually met.

Hackers such as the Data-stream Cowboy are natural computer geniuses. After the age of 20, which seems to be the point when many cast aside their hacking inclinations, some of them move from poacher to gamekeeper and earn large sums of money working as experts on computer fraud. Until then, they are dangerous, unpredictable and difficult to catch: it took some of the finest computer experts in America two years to track down and capture Kevin Mitnick, considered by many to be the ultimate hacker.

The technology the hacker needs is basic: a simple computer, a modem, and some easily obtainable knowledge that can be picked up from the Internet or any of the dozens of hackers' magazines in Europe and America. First, the hacker calls up the computer via a modem to see if there is any easy way to get access to the files or information stored within. If the first attempt fails, there is often a 'back door' to the computer which the hacker can check, but the methods used by hackers to gain access to their prey will vary enormously. Some may keep checking to see whether a particular secret 'door' allowing access to a corporate or government computer has been left open accidentally by its previous user, while others will quietly pick the lock. Kevin Mitnick would overload a computer's defences until it collapsed and he could worm his way inside.

This 64-bit computer chip made in 1992 was the world's fastest microprocessor at the time. It had a performance similar to that of a CRAY-1 supercomputer which a decade earlier was being used to design nuclear weapons.

Often it can take just a few seconds to gain access, but sometimes hours, even days, may be needed. What the hacker wants to see on his or her screen is a request or invitation from the target computer asking the hacker to log-on as the operator. The vulnerable computer is simply asking its operator to put in a password, a procedure it will do perhaps a hundred times a day. Guessing a password may take seconds or days, but many computers are delivered to customers with standard factory passwords already installed, and some people do not bother to change them. Hackers' guidebooks list dozens of possible passwords and there are special computer programs which will automatically try millions of word and number combinations until the right one is accepted.

If a company has even vaguely begun to consider their security they will have installed a line of defence at this stage. The hacker might well have only three tries at getting the right password before the failed attempt is automatically brought to the attention of a systems engineer. But, as recent history has shown, this is not much of a defence against a determined hacker, who will eventually find a password, and can then browse freely among the computer's files. Perhaps the invader is spotted by a computer systems engineer, who switches off the modem link – perhaps not. In many cases the hacker roams within the system and does what he wants. If he wishes to rename a file, he can; if he wants to delete a file containing irrecoverable information on a new bomb, or Aids vaccine, he can do that too. The controls are in his hands, and it is the feel of power at a young age that many hackers find addictive.

Proficient hackers can use the first computer they have entered illegally to jump into other computers and thus cover their tracks. Some will go through three or more different computers, sometimes each in a different country, before having a crack at a government or defence computer. And that, for the authorities, is when the real problems begin.

For a large company, the effects of a computer attack can be completely devastating. Criminal gangs have realised the potential for extortion, and a number of financial institutions in the City of London are known to have paid huge sums of money to gangs of blackmailers threatening to destroy the company's computers and therefore its business. There are at least four separate gangs, two of which are based in Russia, and they are thought to have used extortion to secure more than $600 million from company directors.

The blackmail begins with the criminals obtaining all possible information on the mainframe computers of a particular company (a large bank, for example). With the knowledge they gain, the gangs are then able to hack into the bank's computer systems and leave messages for senior officials warning them of the damage they can do to the computers by dropping logic bombs or computer viruses into the bank's computers, or even threatening simply to delete files. In several dozen cases of computer extortion in London, New York and continental Europe, victims have paid up to $20 million each to avoid a potentially catastrophic attack. The traditional secrecy of the banking sector has prevented police forces from fully investigating the problem, and several banks have flatly denied paying off the blackmailers during interviews with police officers, even when the officers have proof that millions of pounds have been paid as 'ransom'.

The Internet now appears to be turning on its creators and threatening the security of defence installations. The banks and finance houses who have paid extortion money may also be suffering indirectly as a result of defence industry research: experts are convinced that some of the criminal gangs blackmailing large firms include former soldiers trained in computer warfare. This is a new type of combat pioneered by the US, which aims to devastate enemy countries by destroying their computer networks. Computer warfare evolved from the realisation that a nuclear bomb would create a massive electromagnetic pulse destroying all microchips and paralysing tanks, ships, aircraft and electricity supplies. (During the Gulf War several senior American generals wanted to explode a nuclear device above Iraqi troops to knock out much of their fighting capability.)

The Pentagon and the British Ministry of Defence are believed to have developed portable high intensity radio frequency (HIRF) guns that fire electromagnetic pulses, destroying computers within a small radius. Several officials within the FBI and the British government have speculated privately that terrorists may already have managed to obtain one of the HIRF weapons and used it to blackmail banks and financial institutions.

The British police have pioneered the investigation of computer crimes – extortion, hacking and viruses – but they are often obstructed in their work by senior directors of large firms worried about the impact on shareholders of news that the firm is vulnerable to a computer attack, or, even worse, that it has paid millions to Russian blackmailers. But the 'cyber-cops', as they were bound to be nicknamed, are watching closely for the terrorists and blackmailers. "We have seen a huge growth in computer crimes in the last two years, and we believe it is a trend that will continue," said one computer-crimes investigator. "Hacking is becoming much more of a commercial activity, with individuals who used to gain access to sensitive computer files just for fun or a challenge realising they can actually make a large amount of money by using whatever they find for the purpose of blackmail or even selling it if they find information on somebody who is well-known to the public."

THE COMPUTER CRIMINAL of the future will be a stealthy kind of burglar, infinitely more difficult to catch than a housebreaker or armed robber. Instead, they will be hackers or computer scientists who can break into a company's mainframe computer, dig out some useful information and then escape into the anonymity of cyberspace before anyone realises what they have done. The real money is no longer accessible through a safe-deposit vault in your local bank; it is humming along computer wires, passing from account to account through a network of machines which link the entire banking community. Criminals will reach out and grab what they want. There have already been a number of cases where computer criminals have managed to steal millions of dollars from large banks by using computers, and the losses have not even been discovered until accountants have checked the books several weeks or months later.

In one recent British case, a bank clerk who claimed he had been threatened by a gang hacked into his company computer and proceeded to transfer more than £31 million into a Swiss bank account. The crime was only spotted because the bank could transfer a maximum of £30 million, and investigators quickly began searching for the culprit. It was partly luck that the clerk was caught, because some of his colleagues remembered he had been in an area of the bank for which he had no authorisation on the day of the illegal transfer. The police believe the clerk was merely a 'mechanic' in the case, and a criminal gang, possibly foreign, was the driving force behind the crime.

Police forces around the world are now convinced that one of the major threats to international security is coming from organised gangs of Russian computer experts. Disillusioned with their lot under the post-communist regime, dozens of former military computer scientists are believed to have been recruited by the Russian Mafia to hack into the computers of western finance houses, looking for information or money. The Internet and the global computer networks have become the high seas of the twentieth century, and they are populated by a threatening new breed of pirate whose booty is information.

Chapter Ten

DEFUSING THE BOMB

As we complete this book in September 1996, there are signs that the media, with its fascination for horror stories and predictions of doom, is beginning to appreciate the full potential of the millennium bomb. Hitherto the lack of publicity has been one of the key reasons that computer-users and company bosses have not been galvanised into action. Senior management need to ask hard questions of their systems managers, but they also need some knowledge of the problem before they can judge whether they are getting the right answers.

The experts unanimously agree that the problem has to be discussed and debated openly if there is to be any hope of fixing it in time to enjoy the start of a new century. However there remains a widespread attitude in many firms that if they keep quiet about their millennium problems they will avoid embarrassing the company and lowering it in the eyes of its shareholders and customers. After all, who could trust and respect a firm that has failed to prepare for a problem that has been known about since computers were first developed?

Some firms who are taking action may try to 'get one over' on their competitors and gain some degree of business advantage. But in an age of inter-dependency it is ridiculous to imagine companies can exist on their own. If enough firms are crippled by the effects of millennium bugs, everyone will suffer.

Successful communication is therefore one of the keys to solving the problem, and to this end the American and British governments are ordering advisors to warn business and the public of the risks of inaction. * They are also beginning to offer advice about various possible remedies.

Evidence shows America is ahead of Europe and the rest of the world in analysing the glitch and starting to fix it, but Britain is catching up quickly. The government has invited in business leaders, gently warned them of the risks they face, and told them to go away and 'assess their exposure' or 'investigate the problem'.

But even now, just a few years before bugs could damage entire economies, the level of inaction on both sides of the Atlantic is worrying. According to some official surveys and independent research 75 per cent of North American companies, 90 per cent of British, 95 per cent of European and 99 per cent of those in Asia have done absolutely nothing to repair their computers and their software.

They may well think they still have

*Governments also need to remind companies that the year 2000 is a leap year, so they will need to program their computers to cope with an extra day: every four years dozens of crucial computer systems crash collapse because part of their software has 'forgotten' to account for an extra day on February 29th. In 1996 a charity in London lost vital data while computers in at least 16 European and American hospitals went 'off-line'.

time to catch up but unless that opinion is based on professional advice, a rude awakening may be imminent. Senior commercial lawyers and government advisers are suggesting that auditors, who independently examine the financial health of companies and report on their findings to shareholders, will have to start making amendments to annual reports indicating the expected level of danger posed by the Year 2000 problem. Companies that have made no preparations could get an adverse report, which will undoubtedly affect the company's share prices.

It is even suggested auditors will have to give a 'probability of survival rating' to companies (for example, 'Company X will have a 30 per cent chance of surviving beyond the millennium'), because it is feared shareholders may resort to litigation if auditors fail to warn them of a serious business danger which, with hindsight, has been known about for 25 years.

Chris Relleen, general audit partner in the retail and multinational division of Coopers & Lybrand, has recognised the potential danger. His firm is one of the 'big-three' auditors in Britain and handles the accounts of a quarter of the largest FT-SE 100 companies. It cannot afford to ignore the impact of the millennium bomb on its own business and those of its clients. "We are just beginning to look at this," he said. "It seems like such a ridiculous problem, but a number of my companies are saying to me that they are going to have to spend large sums of money on this and they need to explain it to their shareholders."

According to Relleen most companies have only just woken up to this problem within the last 6-12 months: "There is not much future benefit from this and criticism may come when people can see the size of the figures. If companies don't address this issue then there is the potential for all their systems suddenly stopping on New Years Eve 1999; it is a horrifying concept. Most companies are finding this will cost them a lot more than they originally thought." The form of any comment in audit reports is still subject to debate, said Relleen, "but a number of my companies are saying that every company in Britain should be accounting for this and are proposing that the Urgent Issues Taskforce (UIT) at the Accounting Standards Board consider it immediately."

He said the counterpart of the UIT in the US has already prepared a pro forma 'statement of explanation': "There is a view that there is a need for uniformity but whether that will go as far as telling shareholders everything, including how much a company will have to spend, remains to be seen and worked out. However any self respecting auditor and their client would want to let their shareholders know about this. There is now going to be a lot of pressure on companies. Nobody wants to own up to the problem first but companies will have to explain the problem. I have heard a number of directors saying they are going to have to spend huge amounts to fix this."

ANY BRIEF explanation of the millennium bomb at a dinner party, elicits the same response: "Well, presumably they can fix it?". The answer of course is yes...and no; some computers can be fixed, and others cannot. The glitch can be everywhere or nowhere, and the glitch-busters often find no two programs are the same.

But what can actually be done about the millennium bomb? If one has a software editing program, it is possible to read through lines of code and add the numerals '19' in front of the two-digit code for the year. But one needs to have the expertise to fiddle around with computer codes, and few normal users have that ability.

Many politicians and chief executives are clinging to the belief that a company will invent some sort of 'silver bullet' to cure all computers using software programs. Although a firm which develops such a product would be able to capture an incredibly lucrative market, the experts agree that no such tool has yet been found to do a complete job.

A variety of software programs are available that can be 'fed' into the larger, victim computer to track down and modify the dates. But even the most advanced tools that have been developed by companies offering 'millennium solutions' are still making hundreds of mistakes, any one of which could cause the computer to go haywire on New Year's Day in the year 2000.

Short of allowing our societies to revert back to the type of subsistence economy proposed by many of those fundamentally opposed to the computer age, the only recourse is to call on the help of the specialist teams of computer-doctors who have opened companies offering help and advice to those firms with millennium bugs. Millennium UK, based in Bournemouth, southern England, are one of the teams which will benefit from the computer problems by saving other companies from total collapse. Brad Collier, the man who warned his local member of parliament, David Atkinson, of the danger in late 1995, is reluctant to name his clients because of their desire for confidentiality, but Millennium UK is known to be working with at least 20 of the largest British firms, as well as companies and organisations as far afield as Budapest and Helsinki.

The firm's consultants, who are all highly experienced in software troubleshooting, use a combination of computerised software program tools and manually searching through the lines of code to modify them. Collier said that once a company is 'educated' as to the best ways of fixing the problem, consultants can often step back and just gently guide them in the right direction. Occasionally consultants find staff of a client firm suspicious, if not slightly hostile. "It can be quite difficult," said one computer-doctor. "They do not like an 'outsider' coming in to play with their baby."

In the next few years hundreds of thousands of firms around the world will need to be visited by experts who can offer help. Dr Massimo Spalla, an Italian engineer working for Andersen Consulting from a glamorous location in the south of France, races across Europe and the Middle East to help his clients. He predicts that his business will grow quickly within the next few years. With scarce skills, such consultants are now able to charge high rates and the cost of employing a small team could soon run into the millions of pounds. The 'smart money' is already quietly moving into such consultancies, and the international investor George Soros is rumoured to have invested $12 million in one of the leading American firms.

In August 1996, JP Morgan, one of the world's leading banks, advised investors to buy shares in companies offering 'millennium solutions'. According to William Rabin, a senior analyst, the computer industry is "heading for an event more devastating than a car crash". His report for JP Morgan clients was entitled '$200billion? You must be kidding!' It went on: "Although most corporations have not even audited their internal systems to determine how large a problem they have, and revenues and earnings are not expected to ramp up at contract programming companies until next year, investors should start picking their favourite stocks now."

Investors are not the type of people to need telling twice, and they only need to look at the astonishing performance of a basket of shares held in some of the American consultancies to realise their initial investment could grow rapidly over the next few years.

As the risks from the bugs become more obvious, governments and manufacturers are becoming increasingly concerned. Michael Heseltine, the British deputy Prime Minister, has ordered government departments to investigate the extent of the problem and report back on their findings. The Central Communications and Telecommunications Agency (CCTA) has been tasked with raising awareness of the problem within government departments and find quick fixes. It is also responsible for advising the Department for Trade and Industry, which in turn advises British companies and sends warning letters to industrial and commercial chiefs. American business leaders are receiving similar letters from federal departments.

It is difficult to see how any business could fail to heed the danger signs – letters from the DTI or the US government warning of the imminent collapse of entire business sectors are hardly common. To add to the campaign the CCTA has also opened a site on the Internet, under the headline "The millennium bomb" It contains an illustration of an old-style timebomb like a large football and a lighted fuse. It is dramatic stuff, and the CCTA warns: "The costs of making systems Millennium compliant could be huge; the consequences of failing to do so could be disastrous. The major drawback is that this work has an absolute, immovable, completion deadline. If you are able to run your business processing through into the next Millennium you need to rapidly get to grips with this problem."

The CCTA has also set up a millennium bomb discussion group and it organises conferences to help companies suffering similar problems to share experiences. Firms are bound to find the costs affecting their profitability with a consequent impact on tax revenue, and so the Government has a vested interest in offering a hand. However, it is fast becoming a major political issue. "We want to know whether this Government is willing to devote the costs now or whether they are tempted to put it off until after the election for us to deal with," said Geoff Hoon, Labour member of parliament and party spokesman on technology.

IN AMERICA the Clinton administration has set-up a Federal interagency committee to co-ordinate action on the problem. It is chaired by Kathleen Adams, a senior executive within the Department of Social Security, who is leading dozens of meetings and discussions to formulate a proper approach to tackling the glitch and finding cures. But there is no Federal policy or any serious government initiative to warn business and the public of the risks posed by the new millennium. Perhaps they conclude that a company which cannot predict the effect of the Year 2000 does not deserve to stay in business.

The Pentagon is working hard to fix the problem and help others. "In the Department of Defense we are dramatically raising the awareness of the Year 2000 problem across the board, from the department's senior leadership to its systems personnel and its suppliers in the commercial sector," said Assistant Secretary Emmett Paige. "We have set in motion a campaign to find and fix the problem in our weapons systems and automated business information systems. We are also working with other Federal agencies and private industry to increase awareness and solve this ubiquitous problem."

The Pentagon is implementing Year 2000 solutions in each of departments and agencies. "My office is working to facilitate the sharing of Year 2000 information," said Paige, "such as lessons learned, best practices, and status of activities. We must avoid duplication of effort as much as possible."

Each of the three military departments and the two largest defence agencies have established secret Year 2000 'pages' on the Internet for worried army or airforce officers to look at and obtain advice. However, civilians are not able to view them, and it is not possible to check whether there are warnings about the safety of intercontinental ballistic missiles or weapon control systems.

According to the Pentagon, the defence information technology community is very much aware of the date problems and the Department of Defense is now trying to raise the awareness among its 'customers' – senior generals and officers – and 'the entire warfighting community'. "We have made several recommendations that are being acted upon to help the Federal sector address Year 2000 problems," said Paige. "We have implemented Year 2000 solutions in some of our systems, already. In other systems, we are planning the work as part of the normal operations and maintenance cycle. As far as what is possible or should be possible, solutions are being found by the DoD's central design activities as a normal part of their operations and maintenance activities."

Rather worryingly, Paige said that the Pentagon's finance and accounting service has been working on the Year 2000 problem for a number of years, and other military departments will now need to prioritise their work efforts to "get the most critical things done within the resources available". He also admitted that the Pentagon is still assessing where Year 2000 problems exist in the majority of defence systems and trying to determine the resources that are required to solve problems. So the free world can sleep easy in their beds at night: the American military have been fixing their finance and accounting computers of the largest cock-up in history, but have not even begun to look at many missile launching systems or rocket control computers.

At a state level in America, no administration has moved as quickly as that of Nebraska, where – as we have already seen – Governor Ben Nelson is diverting money from cigarette taxes to pay for the $30 million worth of changes. "The cigarette taxes that the state collects have previously been used for infrastructure projects such as capital improvements – rebuilding, etc. What I proposed recently was that a percentage of the cigarette taxes be diverted from that program to the year 2000 problem," said the Governor, who views computers as 'a vital part of the infrastructure'.

"I'm quite proud that we were one of the first to spot the problem and get working on it," said Nelson. "It is obviously a problem and we have been working on it for more than a year, ever since Rod Armstrong, the state technology co-ordinator, first warned me of the dangers. I formed a technology cabinet comprising both private and public individuals who have significant technology needs, in order to pull them together and get them to offer advice. This is a significant problem for us with a potential $30 million cost and I wanted to be out in front; we were faced with the same problem that many governments around the world are facing: we don't have any new revenue resources and without raising taxes I was looking for a way to re-divert money and pay for the problem that was not anticipated ten years ago." The Governor is modest – the problem was hardly countenanced a couple of years ago, and he would have every right to be proud of what he admits is a "novel approach".

Few organisations have already fixed their computers but one that has is Meriter Hospital in Madison, Wisconsin. As already reported, it spotted the problem three years ago and is well advanced. "We knew the problem was coming, programmers have been joking about it for years," said Harris Lemberg, a computer troubleshooter at the hospital. "It was more of a management problem than a technical problem. Actually changing the codes is relatively easy, it's just a problem with throwing enough manpower at the task.

"We physically changed some of the codes by hand, and we also fed computer software into our machines which 'looked' through the lines of code and analysed our data to determine the level of risk and also changed some of the date codes. It took us about two years to go through thousands of programs and we had to go through them all one by one."

Lemberg suggests that other computer-doctors might like to try various different ways of attacking the problem: "If you approach it from your master files rather than through the data files then you can eliminate the need to check many of them because they will not really be at risk." Apart from that, he says, you have to just keep "plugging away" at the problem until it's fixed.

THE EUROPEAN Commission, meanwhile, appears woefully behind in its millennium preparations, and was only warned of the problem towards the end of June 1996 by Britain's Science Minister, Ian Taylor. Since then Martin Bangemann, the EC's Commissioner for Industry, has announced an EC investigation into the problem, and said he planned to meet leaders of business and industry to warn them of the risks.

But how seriously is the European Commission taking the threat of computer chaos? There is a glimmer of awareness according to minutes of a meeting of its Telecommunications Council on 27th June 1996 in Luxembourg. Point eight, said: "At lunch the Council discussed the problems posed by the turn of the century for information technology systems. Wherever a unique indication of the year is required, the use of an abbreviated two digit indication is no longer acceptable, and instead the full four digit representation will have to be used, e.g. 1996 instead of 96.

"Changing the software, and where necessary also the data, represents a major effort. In particular, administrative, financial and accounting applications will be affected, in public administration as well as in the private sector. Furthermore, it will have to be feared that not all problems will, or even can be pinpointed before they appear, and therefore some disruption and artefacts have to be foreseen for the beginning of the next century." The Council then asked the Commission to convoke a group of experts in order to analyse the problem further." However there appeared to be no sense of urgency. Europeans will be rightly angry if the Commission does not move more quickly. On Britain's behalf, Ian Taylor, the minister for science, was scathing of such apparent apathy. "The dog isn't barking and the silence is extremely worrying," he said.

Fortunately, some of the larger European businesses are starting to fix their computers, including Banque Nationale de Paris which is tackling the problem 'gradually', and Electricité de France which has already debugged computers dealing with salaries and pensions. In Holland, where the cost of fixes has been put as high as $200 million by Eindhoven University of Technology, PTT Telecom, the main phone operator, has 220,000 computer programs that must be checked. BSO/Origin, a Dutch software firm already has 30 consultants and plans to bring the number up to 100.

The millennium bomb is an enormous problem for less developed countries where there are many older computers donated by Western nations and businesses. But it also provides opportunities. Many have experienced programmers available at lower rates than are charged in the West. India, the Philippines and other countries in the Far East expect to benefit and, already, Western companies have moved in. Locally-hired staff are used to manually search through lines of computer code looking for the date commands in software downloaded by modem. A further attraction is their experience in outmoded software languages like COBOL.

IBM has opened a base in Bangalore in India, and Andersen Consulting, one of the leading international Year-2000 specialists, is establishing what it has termed a 'solution centre' in the Philippines. Over 1,000 programmers will be working in teams around clock. Each project is expected to take several months and the debugged software will be put through an exhaustive testing process. The teams can also dissect a computer program in, say, Leeds in northern England, via modem from their Philippines nerve centre, tapping keyboards and fixing the glitch overnight when the computers are not in use.

Analysts estimate there are 74 Indian software companies offering solutions to the Year 2000 problem for other firms around the globe, and the extra business could earn India anything up to $1 billion in one-off earnings. The computer industry there is mushrooming and figures from the National Association of Software and Service Companies (NASSCOM) show the country is becoming a world leader in providing software and software services, especially to America, which comprises nearly 60 per cent of exports. In 1995-6 annual turnover was up 61 per cent to 1.2 billion dollars and the sector currently employs approximately 120,000 people in more than 700 firms, of which more than 400 have overseas contracts. In 1985 there were only 6,800 employed in the industry and even in 1990 there were still only 56,000. According to Dewang Mehta, NASSCOM's executive director, more than 100 of the top 500 American companies are already taking advantage of the services provided by Indian software firms.

By 'out-sourcing' or transferring their millennium work to countries where programmers work for lower rates, firms can lower the costs of fixing the millennium bomb. Consolidated Edison of New York, for example, plans to use programmers in Ireland and India. Abe Lichtig, a technical specialist at the electricity firm, which has about three million customers in New York and Westchester County, told Computerworld in April 1996 that the price his firm will be paying to have programs checked and changed overseas is about three times less than they would have been charged by American computer-doctors. Lichtig estimates that if no action is taken about 80-90 per cent of Consolidated's computers would come to a halt at the end of the decade. He believes the Irish and Indian firms provide the maximum experience at the lowest cost. The 'benefits' of the glitch are already being seen in Ireland, where Data Dimensions, a US software company, is recruiting 140 staff for a new millennium software centre in Galway.

BUT WHO can be blamed? It is predicted many firms will consider taking legal action against the companies which built and supplied their computers, and their software, on the grounds that they have failed to provide products 'fit for the purpose', and which are now about to go haywire after just a few years use. "The first thing the board said when I told them of the problem was: 'OK, who can we sue?'," said the Information Technology director for one Australian bank.

This line of action would be fraught with problems, however, because companies and the government will have to rely on some of these same firms for help if they are to have a chance of fixing the problem. But that level of assistance will vary from firm to firm: IBM has admitted they do not have enough programmers to modify all the computers they have supplied over the years with bugs. It means many of IBM's loyal customers "are on their own".

If that is a typical response from a large computer company, what will the smaller ones do? How can customers be sure that they will honour warranties and modify the machines? The truth is, customers cannot be sure, and many experts believe that some of the smaller computer suppliers will go bankrupt within the next few years to avoid any litigation.

According to Professor Richard Susskind of Masons, a leading firm of solicitors in the City of London, the Year 2000 problem is 'quite astonishing' and throws up complex legal issues. "There is already a lot of legal activity on this problem," he noted. "There are lots of legal issues tucked away here, we have done quite a lot of internal research on it and we are considering a variety of ways of publicising the problem," he said. "Company decision makers have a couple of fundamental questions to ask about how this affects their business and who is going to pay to make it right. The first question is not really a legal question, although the investigation into how it affects your business might be time-consuming and costly and you might want to pass the costs on to someone else.

"The second question, if your systems aren't compliant, does involve some legal issues and questions," said Susskind, a highly-respected lawyer who has advised Lord Woolf, the most senior British civil judge on the future of the legal system and the implications for the law of new advances in information technology. "One of the most amazing things about this is that we don't really know the scale of the problem, and to not know the scale of such a potentially large problem is in itself quite astonishing. I was talking to the chairman of one major British building society who was saying that to make just their main systems millennium-compliant is going to take them dozens of man years of effort, and even if firms get their systems worked out, it doesn't mean they can rely on data from other companies." His investigations have already discovered that many firms which developed computer systems for clients in the 1970s have since gone out of business: "Who pays the bill when that happens?" he asked.

The main area of legal debate will centre on whether a computer that was supplied many years ago should have been made millennium-friendly. Susskind said: "For many systems that were developed a number of years ago it could be argued that neither party would have imagined that the computers would last for 25 years, and so given that was not a reasonable expectation it would be hard to pass on liability. However for those systems which it was clear would have a long shelf-life then liability can be considered." Each case will probably have to be taken on its own merits, but there can be little doubt that courts around the world will soon have to decide a date after which all computers should have been built and supplied capable of surviving the millennium.

Peter Bullock, a partner in Masons Information & Technology department, believes that any litigation will take a long time to come to court. "The courts are going to have to decide on an individual case basis by looking at a particular incident and the piece of software that is causing a problem and deciding whether it is unreasonable for the manufacturers not have foreseen it." He believes that users who want recompense from suppliers should group together and put pressure on suppliers to produce one response. "At the moment people seem to be running out of time for checking the lines of code, they won't be able to do it in time," Bullock said. "Before 2000 there will be lots of jumping up and down as we see systems crashing."

But for those companies searching for someone – anyone – to pay for all this work there is bad news from the insurance companies. According to Phil Ward from the Association of British Insurers the millennium bomb is 'an uninsurable problem'. "Firms are not going to be able to put this on their insurance," he said. "They have known about the problem for decades, and they should have considered it long ago."

Chapter Eleven

EURO-CHAOS INTERVENES

There is a crucial problem facing European business that could prevent firms from fixing their millennium bugs which has so far received little consideration – European Monetary Union (EMU) – the plan for all the countries of Europe to adopt the same currency, to be known as the 'Euro'.

The Euro will be worth an entirely different amount to the pound, franc or the mark and across the Continent, banks, businesses and financial institutions will need to change their computers and technology to cope with EMU. As if defusing millions of date-bombs in the next couple of years was not challenge enough, EMU will further put a further strain on the resources of the computer industry.

As the clocks tick on towards the year 2000, and all the problems of the millennium bomb, there will also be an urgent need to reprogram tens of thousands of computers dealing with everything from stocks and shares, payment systems and computers which settle accounts on the money markets, to hole-in-the-wall cash machines on our high streets. As we have already seen, there are not enough programmers to cope with the changes needed for the millennium, let alone when the problem is compounded by the need for many to work simultaneously on preparations for the controversial currency revolution.

In early September 1996, the British government's Taskforce 2000 re-stressed the danger posed by the millennium bomb and also warned that EMU would put a further strain on the scarce human resources. At its London press conference, Peter de Jager, who has been taken on as a special adviser, said: "European Monetary Union will not go ahead because of this problem. That is nothing to do with political opinions, it is just the size of the task."

According to senior members of the Taskforce, there is 'barely' enough time to deal with the Year 2000 issue and 'no time left to do EMU as well'. "I do believe that organisations on the data processing side will be extremely challenged by tackling EMU and the Year 2000 at the same time," said Nick Jones from the Taskforce. "It is a nightmare scenario. Life would be a lot easier for them if EMU did not happen before 2000."

THE WHOLE issue of EMU and the possible costs of its introduction are further confused for British industry and commerce by the rowdy nature of the political debate about the benefits or otherwise of Britain's membership of the European Union. Whether it is a wonderful idea that will revolutionise and revitalise European business, or whether it is a threat to national sovereignty and a wicked ploy by dastardly foreigners to take over Britain, are questions that divide the country. It is also dividing boardrooms which need to take difficult decisions about expenditure.

Do they invest billions of pounds in modifying their computers to accommodate the Euro – with the inevitable risk that Britain will actually refuse to adopt a single currency with a resulting waste of shareholder's money? Alternatively, do they ignore the task and blithely continue with their normal business, only for the nation to suddenly decide that EMU offers them huge opportunities for business and tourism and, yes, they would quite like to join a single currency in 1999. The banks would then have just months to conduct a mammoth re-vamp of their computer system.

"It would be impossible to complete such a massive project in just a few months," said the head of computing at one British bank. "We decided to start preparing now. It was a very tough decision for the board to have to take, but we looked at it logically and decided that it is highly unlikely Britain could afford to sit outside Europe while the rest of the Continent uses the same currency. We will have to join EMU, it is just a matter of timing, so my feeling is that we have to start our planning right now. We cannot leave it any longer, and we certainly cannot leave it another year: it's just too large a task and we do not have enough specialist staff."

"We know that EMU will cause us huge problems, but what we don't know is whether or not we are actually going to participate. It could be rather like suddenly finding you're running in the Olympic 100m final a day before the race," said one bank official.

THE PROBLEMS posed by EMU are already worrying bureaucrats in the EU's headquarters in Brussels but such is the enthusiasm for the new money that few are prepared to admit the logistics of its introduction are unachievable. The British Bankers' Association, which represents more than 300 member institutions in over 60 countries, recently gave evidence to a House of Lords Committee warning that the move to EMU and the introduction of a single currency "constitute major change, which will affect existing financial and economic relationships and behaviour". The report continued: "If the European Union and each individual member states are to retain their competitiveness in world markets then the transition to a single currency must aim to provide minimum disruption to markets and customers". It called for a structured approach and proper planning.

But at the moment, many critics say there is no clear leadership, and it is highly debatable whether the banks will organise themselves in a co-ordinated fashion. The BBA also admitted that co-ordinating the work will be a complex challenge, "particularly given the interdependencies of economic activity which mean that preparations cannot always be run in parallel, but may be consequent upon one another. It is essential that leadership is provided and that there is suitable co-ordination across all sectors of the economy."

In guarded terms, the banks were clearly apprehensive about the modifications they might need to make. Should they amend all bank statements so that balances can be seen in the national currency as well as the Euro? Will cash machines need to handle more than one currency? Will customers of cash machines be able to specify whether they want to withdraw money in their national currency or the currency of Europe? Such practicalities are only just being considered.

Malcolm Levitt, a European Union adviser to Barclays Bank in London, was one of the first to draw attention to the more prosaic and practical difficulties of monetary union, and he now chairs a City of London working group on the implications for the large City financial institutions. "It is a massive information technology project," he said. "Broadly speaking the costs will amount to about £1 billion. We don't know whether the UK will join the system or not, but what we do know is that if it happens we have no choice but to be ready for the Euro." He admitted to a degree of concern about the millennium bomb: "We have always been aware that there could be problems because of the clash with the Year 2000 computer changes."

The resulting difficulties will affect us all. Professor Charles

Goodheart, an EMU expert at the London School of Economics, said: "It is not just the impact on the banks but the impact on everyone else. Outside the banking world not a great deal of research has been done on the inevitable costs. In my view the estimates that have been made about the costs of the changeover are a considerable underestimate. However any change has costs and if we take a short term view then nobody would ever do anything."

An editorial in Computer Weekly in April 1996 discussed the question of the millennium bug by telling a joke: "What have BSE [Mad Cow Disease] and the year 2000 got in common? Answer: Government ministers are aware of the problem and says it's not an issue." The editorial commentary went on to give its readers this warning: "Watch out – an even bigger problem is looming. The changes that will have to be made to IT systems if they are to cope with EMU will make the Year 2000 changes seem a doddle.

"The conversion will be up to two orders of magnitude greater, it will affect many more fields than simply the date, it will be much more difficult to test, and will probably have to be implemented in a much tighter time frame than the year 2000 changes. Moreover, the single currency unit is a European problem, and is not as burning an issue for US-based software suppliers as the year 2000." The magazine concluded: "While many suppliers and consultants are beginning to view the problem as a potential money spinner, only a handful of banks in the UK and Ireland are showing much concern about the problem, and awareness among senior managers is low. Now is the time to prepare."

SOME EUROPEAN companies are already taking action: in Germany, a large taskforce working for Deutsche Bank AG has identified at least 3,500 separate tasks its employer must complete if it is to be ready for EMU in 1999. The Germans appreciate just how much work needs to be done and have even started considering the eventual cost of changing the computers. Astonishingly, the cost to the Dresdner Bank alone has been estimated at around £900 million.

In Britain there is still some confusion about the possible costs, with an initial estimate for UK banks of just under £1 billion. The figure, from the BBA, has been heavily criticised by many other experts who fear it will be much higher. "The most conservative estimates of the cost of the millennium bomb in Britain put the figure at around £5 billion," said the head of computing at one major British bank. "I would suggest that it is much, much higher, but what ever the cost, it will probably be dwarfed by the cost of changing our computers for EMU. Nobody really seems to realise just how complicated a task it is to fundamentally alter computers and technology to cope with this sort of change."

Within some banks there is growing concern about whether solutions for the technological problems caused by EMU can be found. "We are confronted by two logistical tasks which are on a scale we have not had to deal with before," said a senior adviser to one of Britain's largest banks. Like many others we talked to, he did not want to be quoted by name on this contentious issue. According to the adviser both problems have been known about for many years, but they are very different in nature. "With the year 2000, what needs to be done is pretty obvious – there's not much complexity in the subject, just quite a lot of graft.

"With EMU, what needs to be done is less clear because the political masters have not decided what is actually going to happen. There are a lot of unknowns, and we have the problem of dealing in different countries using different languages. We also have instability in the political climates in the member states. This has just gone off the scale as far as risk is concerned."

The advisor said he too anticipates the international banking community will have an even bigger problem with EMU than with making computers 'millennium-compliant'. "One of the biggest problems is the lack of political clarity of what has to be done. EMU is only marginally more complicated than the millennium problem but we are not just talking about banking. Consider the problem of all vending machines: think of how many things take coins, and all of them have to be changed. Think of the horrendous confusion that changing the coins and notes will cause."

"I don't want to be too negative, but re-programming computers might be the least of our difficulties. I have no figures on the cost of EMU [because no organisation appears to have come up with a definitive cost], but I would imagine that the cost would be considerably more than fixing the millennium problem. The change in currency creates a huge number of problems separate to software. Banks have automated teller machines, which would all have to be changed; we also have automated coin handlers, weighing machines, coin sorters and it's likely that we would have to completely change the machines, they're not something we could just send away for the software to be re-programmed. The costs will be astronomical."

The advisor indicated that bank's are annoyed with the politicians for making their task so much harder: if they do not know whether Britain is actually going to enter EMU how can they prepare for the necessary changes? "When we are preparing for EMU we not only have to plan how to move forward, but also how to move backwards if the politicians change their minds," he said. "I understand the need for free trade, but does it really make financial sense to tinker with the currency?" The adviser paused before delivering his most contentious statement: "politicians and senior banking officials do not seem to have budgeted for the sheer physical changes that will be necessary. I am increasingly of the opinion that the cost of EMU will outweigh any later financial benefits."

This raises a crucial question. So far the arguments against EMU have been entirely devoted to political issues, not the economics of the physical changeover. Academics and finance experts who have begun considering the case for and against EMU believe that the European Union must now investigate whether the simple physical shift to a uniform single currency, the re-programming of computers and perhaps the need for entirely new equipment, will cost an impossible sum. According to researchers at the London

School of Economics, it is a question that has not been asked and a debating point that has not yet been considered. However, although nobody is able to provide an estimate of the total cost the scale of the task is obvious, according to Matthew Elderfield, a director of the London Investment Banking Federation, which represents many large banks in the City of London.

"For EMU to be introduced we have come up with at least 63 things that must happen involving 12 different organisations, and each of them needs to cost their bit before we can total up the whole and get some idea an overall figure," he said. "I don't think that anyone has done a cost-benefit analysis of EMU. Our point of view is that this needs to be done."

Elderfield also believes that many of his members will have to prepare for EMU regardless of whether Britain is in or out because they operate internationally. But he says the computer problems do not stop at EMU: "To add fuel to the fire, there are other supervisory requirements that will have implications for computer systems as we head towards 2000." New, highly complicated software installations in the City will also require large amounts of time and manpower. "EMU comes alongside of the Year 2000 problem and all these other new requirements which are major projects in their own right."

Elderfield believes that if all the parameters are decided then there is just enough time to make bank computers ready for EMU in two years, "but if they are not decided then there is a risk that people will not be ready on time, or, more likely, it might be possible to compress the time but the cost will go through the roof and the people who suffer most will be the smaller organisations who don't have the spare budget capacity."

UNFORTUNATELY, Britain is falling well behind France and Germany in the race to prepare for EMU. Many Continental banks have been working on the task enthusiastically for many months, while their British counterparts are still scratching their heads wondering what the future holds. In Germany, the banks signed an agreement with the Bundesbank in April 1996 to use both Euro's and marks in all of their payment systems from the beginning of 1999, while in Britain the Bank of England has only just begun issuing a quarterly bulletin to banks discussing the practicalities.

"The Bank [of England] is telling us what we already know," complained one official from a high-street bank. With the new currency set for introduction in three years, what worried him was the approach of two quite separate computer bombs, and a danger both would detonate. He said that when both issues were examined in conjunction, there was not enough time and he quoted the analysis of the British Bankers' Association: The task would take three years to complete.

Another senior adviser to one of the major European banks suggested the timespan needed is closer to five years. Either way, the huge shortage of skills already predicted by those working to fix the millennium bomb makes it sensible to err on the side of caution. And that raises another argument.

If we are too close to the millennium to revamp all the computers that run Europe's financial system, it seems likely EMU may need to be delayed. This possibility was broached at a conference of 65 European bankers held in May 1996 at Annecy in France and organised by ICL, the British-based computer company.

A straw-poll of the conference delegates showed that two thirds had not even begun to consider the technological implications of EMU – let alone actually started work to modify computers. Only 27 per cent of the bankers polled had plans in place to deal with the huge task, and a mere handful had actually begun work.

Howard Davies, the deputy governor of the Bank of England, attended the conference and told delegates of the need for urgent action to prepare for the changes EMU will require. He admitted to being slightly surprised that some banks have not yet put 'action plans' into place.

So the greatest risk posed by EMU is not to the national sovereignty of Britain, or – for that matter – the sovereignty of Italy or Spain. Its drain on the resources of the computer industry could greatly exacerbate the Year-2000 problem, further reducing the pool of programmers available to re-write software date codes. The worry is that political leaders, committed to the dream of a one-currency Europe, may bully industry and commerce into throwing manpower to make EMU work effectively and at all costs. The resulting chaos would only serve to exacerbate the millennium computer problem. Who says that two bombs never fall in the same spot twice?

Chapter Twelve

IS THERE TIME?

We have seen the size of the millennium bomb, and we have seen the damage it could cause if it explodes. The crucial question must be: can it be defused in time? We face an enormous challenge to apply ourselves collectively to fix a common mistake but still companies deny the problem, ignore the consequences and risk devastation in just a few years time.

Yet the warning from the experts is stark. According to Barry Morgan, the chairman and chief executive of IBM UK: "if you aren't already seriously considering the impact this will have on your business then it is probably too late" – that was a statement delivered in early August 1996 and the clock is still ticking inexorably towards the year 2000. Another statement, from an independent expert: "My own feeling is that we are probably rapidly running out of time and, in many cases, we may have passed the point where there are enough resources and time to fix it," said Professor Keith Bennett, head of the Computer Science Unit at Durham University.

A senior Tokyo-based official from NEC – one of Japan's largest computer companies – said Japan had witnessed similar confusion about dates when the national calendar changed several years ago, but: "it was nothing like this. This time the size of the problem is overwhelming. There are too many computers to deal with."

So just how long can it take to fix the glitch? According to IBM, it could take 400 man years for the average large company to make their systems 'millennium-friendly'. The computer giant says it takes roughly two hours to change each date problem in a program, and with an average of 10 date "elements" needing work in each program, and 20,000-30,000 programs used by the average corporation, it is clearly a huge task. IBM has admitted it has a huge problem with its own computers – let alone those of its clients – and it will only have fixed the bugs in its machines by the middle or end of 1997.

IBM also warns organisations they need to think about how much time they will have to put aside for testing the machines once they appear to be fixed. The testing could be more of a problem than many managers realise. Government advisors and computer experts agree it will require at least a year of continuous work to establish whether all the bugs have been destroyed and the re-written software actually works.

BUT TO fix the bugs programmers first have to 'get inside' the computers. The task is complicated by the existence of passwords, or 'source codes', which can prevent unauthorised programmers from tinkering with corporate computers. Over the years many of the passwords have been mislaid, or the programmers who knew them have left the company. In hundreds of other cases, the passwords are held by outside contractors. A company, for example a bank, may want their computers to perform a series of complex tasks. Rather than build the machine themselves, perhaps because of a lack of expertise, they could tender for a computer company to install the programs, and run and maintain the system. The full burden of worry about the installation is removed from the bank. This practice has worked perfectly well for many years but now, as we get closer to the start of the next century and the millennium bomb problem looms, the bank will want assurances from the outside contractor that the computers they are controlling will be fixed of their glitches. But the contractors will hold the 'source codes' – the keys that provide access to the system – and the bank is completely reliant on them. Some companies which have had their most sophisticated computers installed by outside firms are already finding that normal maintenance agreements do not cover them for debugging work.

"It may seem extraordinary, but some companies which have only recently 'outsourced' their computer operations are facing a huge bill to fix this problem in their computers because the 'outsourcer' is denying responsibility," said one lawyer who did not want to be named because he is acting for a number of clients who have fallen out with contractors. "I can think of similar situations in other areas of business," said the lawyer, "but none of them are on this scale or could result in such a huge cost to the company."

Equally clever lawyers for the 'outsourcers' have scrutinised contracts with a magnifying glass to look for reasons to relinquish responsibility for the problem and, in many cases, have succeeded. The computer user becomes the victim and is then left with a tough decision: Do they work with their outsourcer to fix the problem and pay a huge fee for a job they expected to be covered by their leasing terms? Or, as discussed in Chapter Ten, do they take protracted legal action against them on the grounds they have completely failed to supply machines which are fit for their task.

Like everything associated with the Year-2000 problem, even

this decision is far from simple because of the 'source' codes mentioned earlier: if a company takes legal action against its outsourcer they may refuse to supply the company with the 'passwords' to gain access to computer codes to make the necessary changes.

TO DETERMINE the extent of the Year-2000 problem in British firms, a survey was conducted jointly by the Department for Trade and Industry (the government department that will ultimately have to pick up the pieces if millennium bugs cause chaos for industry), the CSSA (the Computer Services Software Association), the CCTA (who are the main government advisers on computers) and the PA Consulting Group.

Their findings, released in the form of a report garnished with illustrations of old-style bombs with their fuses ignited, make dramatic reading. According to the survey, about 70 per cent of company information technology managers are fully aware of the problem; of which 76 per cent consider the problem to be generally critical or serious. Over 60 per cent expect to be affected before the year 2000 yet "lamentably few" organisations (just 8 per cent) have conducted a full audit. Thirty nine per cent cannot even guess at the costs involved and 52 per cent make 'rough guesses'.

The report provides an estimate of the average cost per company: in excess of £10 million – even more if a company employs the services of millennium-bomb consultants.

So how many senior managers are aware of this problem? According to the report, it was a paltry 15 per cent. "In our opinion," the report's authors warn, "unless specific action is taken immediately, what is currently a manageable problem will become a crisis in 1997/98. Given the simplicity and pervasiveness of the problem, it is inconceivable that organisations will not be affected in some way." The report finishes with a dramatic paragraph which appears designed to make any businessman choke into his coffee: "To ensure your organisation continues in business beyond 2000 your systems need to be millennium compliant. Early action is essential. If everyone leaves it too late, failing to gain access to increasingly scarce resources in 1998 and 1999 could be the undoing of many organisations."

This was extracted from a report – released with the backing of one of the largest British government departments, and one historically reluctant to issue warnings of profound business difficulties in the future – in the middle of 1996, yet companies still ignore the problem. We have already seen that many organisations and companies are experiencing huge difficulties with some of their five-year forecasts, supplies, ordering and so on. How much more evidence do companies need before they start an internal investigation? It is, after all, the public which would ultimately be affected by an economic collapse.

MEETING THE deadline is absolutely crucial. Robin Guenier, the head of Taskforce 2000 – the organisation set-up by the British government to tackle the millennium bomb, warns that the computer industry consistently fails to finish large projects on time and is constantly missing vital deadlines. "This matter is too big, too pervasive and too important to be left to the computer industry," said Guenier, who is the former chief computer adviser to the Cabinet Office and the British government. "In any case, that industry's record for managing the problems and opportunities it has faced so far is not so good. Time and time again it says it can meet a deadline – and, too often, it misjudges the situation and fails to do so."

Guenier is supported in his view by the American computer expert Peter de Jager, who told the congressional committee investigating the glitch earlier this year that the computer industry has a reputation for always missing deadlines. "The facts speak for themselves," said De Jager, pointing to one study of large computer software projects which discovered fewer than 14% of the biggest were delivered on time.

De Jager is particularly concerned about the immovable deadline: "In the past, if we missed a delivery date, we could continue to use what we used yesterday. When the Year 2000 arrives, the programs we used yesterday will be useless. Unless the applications are fixed and available on January 1st, all business will lose the ability to do business."

He continued: "I am at a loss to communicate that message any simpler. Regardless of whether you have a single program to fix, or 75,000 programs to fix, the deadline is the same. You will have heard from some witnesses that you can rest assured they will complete this project on time. This is nothing more than unjustified optimism. If we have any hope of delivering on time in the future, despite our record of delivering late in the past, then we must replace unjustified optimism with determined urgency," he said. "Along with that I wish us luck; we're going to need it."

Professor Bennett of Durham University agrees that the computer industry has a problem with keeping to agreed deadlines: "The computer industry as a whole is one of the worst sectors of industry for keeping to deadlines; not out of malice or mendaciousness, it's just that the industry is not very good at forward-predicting and staying within timescales." What people are working against, said Bennett, is a 'completely immovable deadline'. "I think the problem is as much as anything human management factors, and one of the problems is whether there are enough good managers who can make difficult decisions as project managers. There are simply not enough of them around, and that could be one of the most significant problems when we are trying to tackle this issue."

Robin Guenier was one of the few senior government officials to appreciate the scope of the millennium bomb and it was after a brief presentation by him that Michael Heseltine, the Deputy Prime Minister, ordered a secret government investigation and analysis of the glitch in every department. The results have not been made public, which may suggest to the cynical that Whitehall civil servants are embarrassed at the extent of the problem. When he was given the job of 'saving the nation', as one wag commented, Guenier was provided with the paltry sum of £170,000 to cover the initial start-up funds for his Taskforce 2000. He then had to arrange finance from private business and industry to kick-start the project. A barrister by training , Guenier held senior posts in industry before becoming a consultant, and some have suggested the reason he appreciates the risks of the millennium bomb is precisely because he is not a computer expert, and is not seduced by the computer industry's inflated view of its own genius.

Guenier is now viewed as the millennium bomb expert in senior government circles and has been called upon to brief not only Heseltine but many senior British civil servants. He feels he has got the message across in Whitehall but he remains concerned that computer industry bosses and other business leaders are too ready to accept the suggestion that there are easy solutions. "It would, I suggest, be unwise to accept assurances from the industry that this is not so big a problem. And it has to be said that this is the industry that created the problem and it is only drawing it to our attention at this desperately late hour." Guenier believes it may be unwise to leave the

Robin Guenier, head of Britain's taskforce dealing with the year 2000 problem. He warns of a public backlash against computers.

job of fixing the problem to some senior businessmen. "They may be unwilling to jeopardise this year's bonus by taking a multi-million pound profit reduction now to solve a problem that is over three years away – possibly after they have retired," he said.

Concerns that the problem is still being ignored are reinforced by CMG, a European information technology services group. "This problem is conservatively estimated at costing Britain's leading companies many millions to solve, yet 78 per cent of chief executives are severely underestimating the price or don't know what it will cost at all," said Ian Taylor, its chairman in Britain. When CMG conducted an investigation, 11 per cent of the chief executive's they surveyed were not even aware the problem existed: "Shareholders, customers and employees need to make their voices heard to stimulate a response to a situation which can only get worse."

Taylor suggests looking to America for an example of the need for swift action, perhaps because America is still the only nation where its extent within government departments and agencies has been investigated and made public.

The Congressional subcommittee on government management, information and technology, which is the main political body pushing for action, has checked 24 major government departments and produced some worrying findings. According to Stephen Horn, the subcommittee chairman and a Californian Congressman, the survey shows that Washington is woefully unprepared for millennium bugs. NASA, the US space agency, and the Departments of Energy and Transportation – all supposedly forward-thinking departments – come low down on the Congressional subcommittee's league table for preparedness and ability to cope with the year 2000.

The congressional committee is trying to shame US government departments into action by 'awarding' them grades of A to F. Ironically NASA, viewed as "one of the most innovative and advanced" agencies within the American government and one of the most "computer dependent agencies in the federal government", received a 'D'. And Energy, Labor and Transportation each received an 'F' – back of the class for them..

Why, then, has NASA not prepared a plan for dealing with their millennium bugs? A spokesman in Houston promised to find out but did not return our calls. NASA apparently does not anticipate formulating a plan until March 1997 but as we have already seen, with most computer experts estimating that companies and organisations need to put aside approximately a year and a half to test computer systems after they appear to have been cleared of their Year 2000 bugs, that will leave just a year for NASA to act. Can they complete such a Herculean task in time? It will certainly require an enormous effort, and many other computer experts are highly critical of NASA's 'dangerous' inaction: "I find their lack of concern quite astonishing," said an official from a department which works closely with NASA. "This problem will affect the agency particularly badly but they are completely relaxed. They seem to be so busy looking at the heavens that they have forgotten what goes on down here on earth."

But the congressional subcommittee does not reserve its criticism solely for those at the bottom of their league table. Those nearer the top are approaching the problem "with a great degree of complacency", according to one comment.

The Social Security Administration, which has been lauded as one of the few organisations to actually start working on the glitch and the Department of Defense – with its estimated 358 million lines of computer code to be checked at a cost of anything up to $3 billion – have both been criticised for not finishing inventories of programs that are at risk from millennium bugs, producing final estimates of the cost of the problem or appointing a single executive who can take overall charge of the task of fixing the glitch. Social Security was, however, still awarded an 'A' grade by the subcommittee for their response to the problem, as were the departments of International Aid, Personnel and Small Business. 'B' grades went to the departments of Education and State.

THE LACK of time available before the end of the millennium is not the only reason companies which have so far failed to start modifying their computers should start to panic. Another huge problem, apart from time, is that there are not enough computer programmers to cope with all the changes that need to be made. IBM put it succinctly: "there are approximately 90,000 programmers in the world who understand COBOL [the old computer language at the heart of many computers infected with millennium bugs]...but we actually need at least two million to fix the problem".

The economics of the situation are simple: there are absolutely crucial changes that must be made to computers, and only a tiny number of specialists capable of performing the work – the result is that the salaries of those computer expert who can read old languages such as COBOL and work on old 'legacy' computers (the ageing systems installed in many large corporations which still run much of the company's operations) will rocket in the next few years.

Some commentators believe that the few who have the vital skills will be able to charge astronomical sums for their time, and there are suggestions that salaries, which in some cases already top £100,000 per annum, could rise to £1,000 per day as we get closer to the end of the decade. According to a report published at the end of 1995 by the Institute of Data Processing Management in Kent, the number of advertised jobs which mention a requirement for an applicant to have COBOL programming skills has increased by 68 per cent over the previous two years. Some companies have already realised they must attract staff with the right skills, and are attempting to tie them into lengthy contracts which will prevent them leaving in the middle of crucial date-change projects.

"I do not believe there are enough people to fix this, definitely not, and that means all of us – including the general public – are facing a serious problem," said Ian Rickwood, the chief executive of Institute of the Data Processing Management, which has 11,000 computer experts as its members. "Even if people are training programmers in places like India– it could be too late for some firms."

Chris Elliott, the marketing director of Dun and Bradstreet Software, has also warned an unprecedented demand could develop for specialists in old computer languages by 1997-98, and he also said it may not be possible to meet the demand by the end of the millennium. Such predictions hardly bolster the belief that the problem will be fixed in time by an army of eager programmers. But then as Robin Guenier says, the optimists have never really considered the full scope of the problem. He believes chief executive's will be crying out for expert staff, and only those companies which can afford to pay extortionate prices will be able to save their computers, and thus their companies.

PERHAPS we should spare a moment to feel sorry for those companies which have made many of their more senior – and older – computers system experts redundant in recent years only to realise they cannot now fix the date codes without their help. Or perhaps not. Some companies have already been forced to re-employ the same people on vastly inflated salaries because they are the only ones who actually understand their old firm's machines.

There are tales, some of them apocryphal, about retired programmers quietly pottering about their gardens pruning rose-beds, only to receive frantic telephone calls from their former managers or replacements asking whether they could return to their old company on a "consultancy" basis. "I am convinced that some 'has-beens', even those in their sixties, will be the only ones who have the necessary skills to fix this problem," said Ian Rickwood from the Institute of Data Processing Management. "Companies will have absolutely no choice but to re-employ them, and their salaries will be high. Many of the most vital staff that are needed to fix this will be in extremely short supply and poaching will inevitably take place, just as it always does when there is a shortage."

Rickwood said the new younger whizkids who run many company computers often do not understand the 'core' of the machine: "We have now got to the stage where some companies cannot access computer data written in old languages and some companies have computers where the core of the machine is so old that it uses languages which very few people understand."

Anyone who 'speaks' the languages would – indeed – be just as useful as a retired systems expert. However many companies are finding the software in their computers, which in many cases is the oldest element, contains bizarre codes and passwords that must be negotiated before the lines of actual code can be checked.

It is reminiscent of how the peoples of the ancient world hid their most precious treasures behind booby-traps and clever devices to protect against intrusion. The 'booby-traps' which some old systems experts installed in their computers take us back to the sociological problem we all have with technology and those who understand computers.

There is an unfounded mystique around computers which leaves many feeling intimidated by those who appear to be able to manipulate the machines with ease. Computer experts have long been left alone within firms to get on with the job of running and maintaining their machines, and many of them have tried to protect their jobs and long-term careers by customising the software so they alone can understand it.

Much of the customisation took place in the 1970s when there was a huge growth of interest in computers. Many specialists realised that a technical revolution was underway, encouraging thousands of new, and cheaper, programmers into the business. Inadvertently, and perhaps not realising the damage they could be causing in the future, they tinkered with software to adapt the computers to the particular needs of their companies. Or they may have represented computer date codes with words to while away the long hours between nine and five each day. The result is that instead of numbers the names of football teams or wives are being discovered throughout some ageing company computers.

It is easy to imagine how such personal modifications could hugely complicate the task facing those who now need to change the date codes. Not only do they have the needle-in-a-haystack task of finding and fixing lines of code, but in many cases they also have to decipher personalised gobbledygook.

"In some cases, particularly in the military, we no longer have the source codes, they can't be re-compiled, the compilers don't exist, there are emulators* built on emulators," said Professor Bennett wearily. [* Emulators 'translate' old code to new so different computers or parts of computers can understand each other]. "So even if one understands where the problem is out there, actually getting to the bottom of it and actually fixing it is going to be a nightmare. I would work on the basis that there are problems. If I were in charge of nuclear control systems I would want to check and know what could happen – immediately."

SO FIXING the problem may not be possible in the time available and the results could be horrendous. If we include all the problems of the stock market, traffic lights, pensions, public transport, and every other glitch we have explored, we are left with a nightmarish vision of a computer-age that has turned on itself and destroyed our society. We could open our eyes on New Years Day and wake to a world that has ceased to function in a way we would recognise. Bleary-eyed and hungover from the festivities of the night before, we could turn on the bathroom tap, but no water comes out because the computerised pumps which control the flow of water have shut-down. We turn on the light switch, but nothing happens, because the electricity grid is down. We pick up the telephone to find out why but there is no dialing tone. Outside, on the street, we meet people walking around enquiring whether their neighbours have running water or electricity.

Maybe the electricity stays on, maybe the traffic lights do not create chaos, and at least some shops have food. But nobody today can say for sure. Not enough work has been done yet by the computer industry to establish which computer programs are at risk: will the millennium bomb cause chaos within this city, or that electricity station, or that hospital? No-one knows...

But if you believe our warnings of chaos in the developed countries, and accept our findings that there is not enough time and too few programmers left to fix the problem by the year 2000, what can you do to limit your personal suffering? Perhaps you should consider moving to Cuba and buying a beachfront property near Havana: the people's republic is one of the least computer-reliant countries in the world. Or perhaps you should take the advice of one American computer programmer who predicts the end of our computerised global economy on a Year 2000 discussion forum on the Internet: "Buy a cabin in the country, and stock up on plenty of beer and ammunition. Then sit tight and wait for civilisation to evolve again."

But out of the possible chaos may emerge scenarios that have not even been considered. The millennium bomb may just be a catalyst for positive change and the way we use computers could be radically altered for our own good.

Chapter Thirteen

MILLENNIUM MELTDOWN

The Year 2000 problem can be solved if billions of lines of new software code are rewritten, tested and installed before 31st December 1999. Some think it can be done, but it is important to consider what could happen if the deadline is not met and there is a global computer 'meltdown'.

The term meltdown came into common usage though the movie 'The China Syndrome' in which enriched uranium fuel rods of a nuclear reactor go out of control. One problem compounds another, the core of the reactor overheats and the molten fuel melts its way through the containment vessel into the earth below.

In terms of the Year 2000 problem it is a vivid description of a disastrous failure. If enough computer systems crash in the early hours of the next century, the complex mechanisms of society, with its intricately connected banking, retailing and trading systems, will suffer a domino collapse. It may sound unlikely but, what if..?

A report sponsored by the British Department of Trade and Industry describes the Year 2000 glitch as "a simple problem with catastrophic consequences". "The change of the millennium reveals a simple flaw present in some form in almost all computers which will cause them to fail," the report warns. "If these computer systems support your key business processes then they too may fail. If your key business processes fail your organisation will more than likely fail. If several organisations fail we face a disaster. If many fail around the world we face a catastrophe."

It could happen. The global economy is presently based upon a concept of continuous expansion through the development and spread of a technology-based infrastructure. Industrialised countries are at the forefront of the growth and they are driven by profit motive realised through their global network of stock and money markets.

Those markets are now all electronically linked by computer and yet more machines control the mechanisms for finance, buying and selling, production, distribution and exchange. Black Monday, the famous 'Crash of 1987', when the Dow share index fell by more than 500 points, demonstrates just how reliant the world's stock and capital markets are on computerised systems which are wholly software dependent - the 1987 stockmarket crash shows the trading bubble in American, European and Asian markets can be burst in minutes by runaway computerised trading.

The computers used in the world of finance and money sit in the offices of stock brokers, on the floors of futures markets and stock exchanges, in banks and in the offices of finance and investment houses, economic consultants and financial journalists. They are connected in an enormous world-wide network and an information infrastructure linking together both the financial decision makers and the mass media. Split-second reactions result in decisions to buy or sell stock.

According to its critics, the basic problem with this electronic trading machine is that it cannot be halted and cannot even 'mark time', instead operating with a sort of perpetual motion. If the computers do not work the whole money market process, and everything dependent upon it, stops.

As markets close at the end of each day, all current holdings have a published value which forms the basis for credit and debit trading. Without computers there can be no such market valuations, and no method of exchanging stocks and shares, foreign currency, domestic cash, government bonds and a thousand other instruments by which wealth is calculated. Ledgers have almost entirely disappeared and only computers hold the records. Assets held at banks, which form the basis of credit and trading, become intangible if their value cannot be found on the computer screen, and this could happen when the new century dawns.

"When people first hear of this they cannot believe it is a serious problem but when one starts to think through the consequences, and the consequences of the consequences, it could be quite enormous," said Professor Keith Bennett of the Computer Science Department at Durham University. "I don't think this has really been thought through because, for example, the banks must consider what will happen to them if their clients start to go bankrupt on a large scale – the multiplier effect will work through the economy. It is a very serious problem with major implications for not only the industry but also the public."

As everyone agrees, neither corporations nor individuals can spend their money or assets if banks cannot present, count or value it. Worse still, the banks may not even be able to provide access to money when the millennium bombs explode because they have made their everyday retail operations computer dependent and intricately connected via computers.

But quite apart from the risks to the global economy, we are now dependent upon computers for basic life processes. We need them to manage urban living because the manner in which we have changed and organised our cities has transformed them during the present century into whirling machines which are extremely vulnerable to failure. The computerised cogs all play their individual part with few humans understanding how they all mesh together.

Phase one of these changes was the mechanising of transport in the last century with the trolley bus, the train, the tram and the automobile replacing horse-drawn vehicles. Then electricity and electronics helped with the automation of large chunks of manufacturing industry. In the third phase we have seen computers replacing humans in watch-keeping, calculating, timing, and decision making. Few things can now be made without a high degree of computerisation, yet the process of change continues apace, often causing rapid social upheaval.

The West's dependence on computers might just have created the conditions for a breakdown – for example, we have seen how the automation of food distribution through supermarkets is highly vulnerable to the millennium bug. Over the last decade, large store chains have moved over to electronic methods of payment at the cash tills, 'electronic fund transfer at point of sale' or EFTPOS.

Plastic cards and computerised money are the most popular method of buying goods, and even people who pay are likely to have used plastic to withdraw the notes from a bank cash machine. But however funds for the purchase are obtained, computers will be checking the customer's credit limit and taking the decision to allow or reject the purchase.

The new 'loyalty discount cards' currently being introduced in stores across Britain, Europe and America, make the process of payment even simpler. A computerised account is set up for the customer by the supermarket into which regular payments are made by direct debit. The stores' computer will monitor the monthly balance and pay interest on any sum that is in credit after each grocery bill is debited. Supermarkets are trying to become banks in their own right, and extensive new software systems have

Life was so much simpler in the 1960s when computers like this monster with its 1,290 dials were used by the US electricity industry.

been developed to handle millions of new customer accounts.

As a number of systems analysts have confided to us, there is concern these new software development projects are taking place at the same time as the millennium bug needs to be tackled. Stores are risking a double software jeopardy in the run up to 2000.

So what happens if the store computers go down on Saturday, January 1, 2000? Many shops cannot operate without a computer systems functioning perfectly. The store would not know what bar code price to put on items it was displaying for sale; it could not recognise the prices of any item it was selling; it could not add up the items in the grocery basket; and it could not present a bill to the customer for payment.

Behind the scenes there would be even more chaos because computers could no longer tell warehouses what stocks to deliver 'just in time' to replenish what has been sold. The food supply chain would rapidly break down, and so would all other supply systems struck down by the bug, including the delivery of fuel to filling stations, industry and the home, another highly automated area.

The problem would be exacerbated if some banks were also experiencing bugs in their software. With ATMs and cash card systems out of action, people might go to their local branches to draw out hard cash. In the rush, the supply of notes would rapidly run out. Recent software failures had similar effects but the banks were unable even to give up-to-date balances. Meltdown means retailing would be in chaos.

Electricity supply is another critical area. Power demand from the national grid and the electricity companies varies widely according to the time of day and whether it is a weekday or a weekend. The peaks of demand are served by rapidly bringing spare oil-fired turbine generators on stream at critical times. Computers monitor power-usage and are programmed to anticipate when these points are approaching. At key reservoirs around the country they can pull the plug on billions of gallons of stored water which rushes down chutes and sets in motion the turbine blades of generators. Without such computerised balancing of supply-demand, there would be power-cuts or voltage would drop to an unacceptably low level – which would, for example, make kettles slow to boil. Such brown-outs are well known in Florida, where the electricity supply is often inadequate to meet demand from air conditioners in sweltering weather. When this happens the supply drops and flickers. Not as serious as black-outs, these are known as 'brown-outs'. But computers cannot handle brown outs, and computer stores in Florida sell a rechargeable battery pack which kicks in automatically if the mains electricity voltage flickers below an acceptable level. Europeans are not so accustomed to power failures and electricity grids are generally more sophisticated.

But if a millennium bug cripples their computer systems, black-outs would be likely. If these were prolonged, even computers with back-up batteries would lose power and fail. It is also clear that communications could be severely jeopardised, further adding to the chaos. Both land-line and cellular telephones are dependent on computer software switching and such computers could shut-down. The accurate positioning of geo-stationary satellites depends on regular computer-generated signals being beamed to them from earth. If they wander off-course, all international telephone traffic would fade out.

These problems would affect the cogs in the machinery of modern society. With transport and communications in chaos, food hard to get, cash unavailable and gas stations out of fuel or subject to long queues of panic buyers, the conditions would be met for a devastating break down. The situation would not be helped when millions of people found they could not get to work because the transport infrastructure had also collapsed. Modern organisations have few spare resources to save the day: just as supply has been organised on the 'just-in-time' principle, staffing is organised according to principle of 'just enough' to get by.

There could be a run on the banks, massive traffic jams, and a rapid depletion of all available fuel supplies. This could be accompanied by the sort of lawlessness, violence, rioting and looting which has on numerous occasions been shown to lurk only just beneath the veneer of civilisation. The mere preservation of law and order might necessitate curfews, rationing and the use of martial law, and there could be long traffic jams as people quit cities for rural locations.

It seems apocalyptic but people were speaking in just these terms at an important press conference in London in September 1996 as this book went to press. It was called by the British Government to publicise the setting up of its Taskforce 2000 and pulled few punches. Members of the taskforce told journalists that three major airlines have already decided to stand down all flights for 24 hours on New Year's Eve 1999 even if their own computers are sorted out in time, because they cannot be sure that other aircraft and air traffic control systems will work correctly.

Taskforce officials pointed out that Global Positioning Systems, which have directed Cruise missiles to their targets, and ships and planes to their destinations, will reset its date to January 6 1980, because of a 2000-related fault. Credit cards with expiry dates in 2000 have already been withdrawn because point of sale machines did not recognise them, they said. Great-grandparents aged 104 had been told to report for school by computers which thought they are four-year-old toddlers. The list of problems seemed unending: Computer files being wiped clean; and silicon chips controlling traffic lights, heating systems, lifts, cash machines and railway systems ceasing to work. According to Nick Land of Taskforce 2000, a senior partner at accountants Ernst & Young, the effects: "Could be minor or they could be catastrophic."

"It is already too late because there is simply not enough time for everyone to fix their computers," said Dave Allen from Logica, the computer services company. "The problem is huge, ranging from central company computer records which could be destroyed or automatically wiped because the computers will think the tape is very old, to the failure of entire military control systems."

According to Allen there are "lots of horror stories" about how American F-14 fighter pilots could suddenly find their missiles arming in the first few minutes of the new millennium and he says: "there is a huge shock horror aspect to all this, but the truth is we just don't know what is going to happen in many areas such as defence and the military."

"WE SPEND our lives preparing for chaos, and hoping it never happens," said the Emergency Planning Officer for one English council. "Society has evolved with technology and it is perfectly possible that we will now need to consider what happens if the computers that run our societies and economies collapse. Civil order must always be maintained, and we have to draw up plans to prepare for all sorts of crises. People think we are just playing games... until things go wrong."

Ironically, in America it is computers that are now being used to deal with civil emergencies. EIS International Corp. has developed software for an emergency planning system which is already being used at 5,000 locations.

James Morentz, the firm's President, claims it can be used to deal with almost any threat from social unrest, trouble at the Olympic Games, or any type of natural and man-made disaster. Prudently, it does not run on mainframes but on a personal computer, which might just be more millennium-friendly. However complete social breakdown and technological failure is likely to be beyond its capabilities.

Our complex social system can slow down for a few days around scheduled public holidays, but these have been anticipated. What has never been anticipated – or planned for – is an unscheduled massive disruption continuing for a long period of time. In these circumstances, a society designed never to stop could grind to a halt, and no-one really knows if it could be restarted.

No-one can be smug, even those companies and administrations which believe their systems have been purged of date-code problems. Modern computer systems are so expensive that few organisations have a 'spare' on which to carry out trials. The start of the new century will be the first opportunity to test these systems under full operating conditions.

When Ian Taylor, the British Science Minister, states that failure to solve the millennium problem could lead to "commercial collapse and international chaos", it is this gloomy scenario that his civil servants have warned him about. It is a possibility, not a prediction, but the world has three years left in which to work to avoid millennium meltdown.

The Millennium Bomb

Index

Index

Index

Index

Index